LAKE DISTRICT LO

Now a UNESCO world heritage site, the Lake D
regions in the United Kingdom. The Ice Age forn
national park is renowned all over the world for it

The lake District, which got its name from the 16 lakes, is a popular tourist destination that attracts up to 16 million tourists in a year. It lures its visitors not only with the beauty of nature but also with its 214 peaks which rise to almost 1000 meters. Some find rest in the lonesome trails while others search for the thrill in the national park. There is a rush of adrenaline when climbing the fells that is unmatched, as confirmed by several hikers.

Surrounded by 2000 meters squared of nature, the lake district is a region with a special charm. Located just South of Scotland with the Irish Sea to the West lies the Lake District, otherwise known as Lakes or Lakeland. It is found in Cumbria, North West England. The lake District is just a 3.5-hour train ride from London. It is also an hour and a half away from Manchester International airport which makes it very accessible to tourists.

The lake District is England's green, pristine mountain playground. Its inhabitants preserve their natural sceneries and their centuries old tradition which maintains the appeal of the popular tourist destination.

Apart from being the home of the most visited national park in the U.K., The Lake District is also very famous for its Wainwrights. Named after Alfred Wainwrights, the name is used to refer to the 214 Fells in Lake District that are especially loved by hikers.

This logbook is equipped with a tick-off list and is designed to help you document and log in your data each time you complete a fell. Each fell has its own page which includes details like accurate OS grid reference for each fell and altitude in feet and meters. There is no better companion for a hiker than this logbook.

LIST OF FELLS
(ASCENDING ORDER)

TRAIL	PAGE	HEIGHT	TRAIL	PAGE	HEIGHT	TRAIL	PAGE	HEIGHT
☐ Castle Crag	4	290 m	☐ Low Pike	46	508 m	☐ Seathwaite Fell	88	601 m
☐ Holme Fell	5	317 m	☐ Beda Fell	47	509 m	☐ High Seat	89	608 m
☐ Black Fell	6	323 m	☐ Hen Comb	48	509 m	☐ Illgill head	90	609 m
☐ Loughrigg Fell	7	335 m	☐ Broom Fell	49	511 m	☐ Heron Pike	91	612 m
☐ Rannerdale Knott	8	355 m	☐ Mellbreak	50	512 m	☐ Great Borne	92	616 m
☐ High Rigg	9	357 m	☐ High Tove	51	515 m	☐ Hartstop Dodd	93	618 m
☐ Sale Fell	10	359 m	☐ Sallows	52	516 m	☐ Birks	94	622 m
☐ Troutbeck Tongue	11	364 m	☐ Whinlatter	53	517 m	☐ Yewbarrow	95	627 m
☐ Latrigg	12	368 m	☐ High Hartstop Dodd	54	519 m	☐ Murgrisdale Common	96	633 m
☐ Ling Fell	13	373 m	☐ Souther Fell	55	522 m	☐ Starling Dodd	97	633 m
☐ Walla Crag	14	379 m	☐ Crag Fell	56	523 m	☐ Little Hart Crag	98	637 m
☐ Hallin Fell	15	388 m	☐ Bonscale Pike	57	524 m	☐ Causey Pike	99	637 m
☐ Silver How	16	395 m	☐ Eagle Crag	58	525 m	☐ Grey Crag	100	638 m
☐ Helm Crag	17	405 m	☐ Gavel Fell	59	526 m	☐ Base Brown	101	646 m
☐ Grange Fell	18	416 m	☐ Great Cockup	60	526 m	☐ Fleetwith Pike	102	649 m
☐ Fellbarrow	19	416 m	☐ Arthur's Pike	61	533 m	☐ Rossett Pike	103	651 m
☐ Gibson Knott	20	420 m	☐ Great Mell Fell	62	537 m	☐ Great Sca Fell	104	651 m
☐ Buckbarrow	21	423 m	☐ Whin Rigg	63	537 m	☐ High Spy	105	653 m
☐ Low Fell	22	423 m	☐ Calf Crag	64	537 m	☐ Harterfell	106	654 m
☐ Steel Knotts	23	432 m	☐ Lank Rigg	65	541 m	☐ Middle Dodd	107	654 m
☐ Arnison Crag	24	433 m	☐ Blea Rigg	66	541 m	☐ Selside Pike	108	655 m
☐ Glenridding Dodd	25	442 m	☐ Hard Knott	67	549 m	☐ Scandale	109	656 m
☐ Binsey	26	447 m	☐ Tarn Crag	68	549 m	☐ Place Fell	110	657 m
☐ Great Crag	27	449 m	☐ Meal Fell	69	550 m	☐ High Pike	111	658 m
☐ Nab Scar	28	450 m	☐ Rosthwaite Fell	70	551 m	☐ Whiteless Pike	112	660 m
☐ Catbells	29	451 m	☐ Lord's Seat	71	317 m	☐ Carrock Fell	113	663 m
☐ Graystones	30	452 m	☐ Steel Fell	72	553 m	☐ Tarn Crag	114	664 m
☐ Barrow	31	455 m	☐ Knott Rigg	73	556 m	☐ Wether Hill	115	671 m
☐ Raven Crag	32	461 m	☐ Brock Crags	74	561 m	☐ Loadpot Hill	116	672 m
☐ Barf	33	468 m	☐ Angletarn Pikes	75	567 m	☐ Scar Crags	117	672 m
☐ Lingmoor Fell	34	470 m	☐ Outerside	76	568 m	☐ Bakestall	118	673 m
☐ Armboth Fell	35	475 m	☐ Sergeant's Crag	77	571 m	☐ Sheffield Pike	119	675 m
☐ Burnbank Fell	36	475 m	☐ Blake Fell	78	573 m	☐ Loft Crag	120	680 m
☐ Gowbarrow Fell	37	481 m	☐ Maiden Moor	79	575 m	☐ Bannerdale Crags	121	683 m
☐ Sour Howes	38	483 m	☐ The Nab	80	576 m	☐ Great Calva	122	690 m
☐ Longlands Fell	39	483 m	☐ Hartstop Above How	81	581 m	☐ Ullock Pike	123	690 m
☐ Baystones	40	487 m	☐ Ard Crags	82	581 m	☐ Seatallan	124	692 m
☐ Grike	41	488 m	☐ Middle Fell	83	582 m	☐ Rest Dodd	125	696 m
☐ Green Crag	42	489 m	☐ Brae Fell	84	586 m	☐ Caw Fell	126	697 m
☐ Dodd	43	502 m	☐ Shipman Knotts	85	587 m	☐ Grey Knotts	127	697 m
☐ Stone Arthur	44	504 m	☐ Bleaberry Fell	86	590 m	☐ Gray Crag	128	699 m
☐ Little Mell Fell	45	505 m	☐ Haystacks	87	597 m	☐ Pavey Ark	129	700 m

LIST OF FELLS

(ASCENDING ORDER)

TRAIL	PAGE	HEIGHT	TRAIL	PAGE	HEIGHT	TRAIL	PAGE	HEIGHT
Cold Pike	130	701 m	Slight Side	160	760 m	Lingmell	189	807 m
Bowscale Fell	131	702 m	High Raise	161	762 m	Steeple	190	819 m
Pike of Blisco	132	705 m	Wetherlam	162	763 m	Hart Crag	191	822 m
Yoke	133	706 m	Stony Cove Pike	163	763 m	Red Pike	192	826 m
Whiteside	134	707 m	Great Rigg	164	766 m	High Street	193	828 m
Pike of Stickle	135	709 m	Hopegill Head	165	770 m	Crag Hill	194	839 m
Knott	136	710 m	Wandope	166	772 m	St Sunday Crag	195	841 m
Branstree	137	713 m	Grey Friar	167	773 m	Scoat Fell	196	841 m
Brandreth	138	715 m	Sail	168	773 m	Stybarrow Dodd	197	843 m
Lonscale Fell	139	715 m	Red Screes	169	776 m	Grasmoor	198	852 m
Birkhouse Moor	140	718 m	Dow Crag	170	778 m	Great Dodd	199	852 m
Froswick	141	720 m	Harter Fell	171	779 m	Dollywaggon Pike	200	858 m
Thunacar Knott	142	723 m	Kidsty Pike	172	780 m	Crinkle Crags	201	859 m
Clough Head	143	726 m	Glaramara	173	783 m	White Side	202	863 m
Ullscarf	144	726 m	Thornthwaite Crag	174	784 m	Skiddaw Little Man	203	865 m
Hindscarth	145	727 m	Great Carrs	175	785 m	Blencathra	204	868 m
Kentmere Pike	146	730 m	Allen Crags	176	785 m	Fairfield	205	873 m
Long Side	147	734 m	Watson's Dodd	177	789 m	Raise	206	883 m
Sergeant Man	148	736 m	Grisedale Pike	178	791 m	Esk Pike	207	885 m
Harrison Stickle	149	736 m	Dove Crag	179	792 m	Catstye Cam	208	890 m
Seat Sandal	150	737 m	Rampsgill Head	180	792 m	Nethermost Pike	209	891 m
Robinson	151	737 m	Brim Fell	181	796 m	Pillar	210	892 m
The Knott	152	739 m	Haycock	182	797 m	Great Gable	211	899 m
High Crag	153	744 m	Green Gable	183	801 m	Bowfell	212	903 m
Carl Side	154	746 m	High Raise	184	802 m	Great End	213	910 m
Dale Head	155	753 m	Kirk Fell	185	802 m	Skiddaw	214	931 m
Red Pike	156	755 m	Swirl How	186	802 m	Helvellyn	215	950 m
Hart Side	157	756 m	Old Man of Coniston	187	802 m	Scafell	216	964 m
Ill Bell	158	757 m	High Stile	188	806 m	Scafell Pike	217	978 m
Mardale Ill Bell	159	760 m						

CASTLE CRAG
290 M (951 FT)

REGION: North Western   OS GRID: NY249159

Date:

Companion:

Weather condition:

Descent start time:

Descent duration

Finish time:

Difficulty:

☆ ☆ ☆ ☆ ☆

Views

☆ ☆ ☆ ☆ ☆

Ascent start time:

Ascent duration:

Peak time:

Rating

☆ ☆ ☆ ☆ ☆

Total Duration:

Total distance:

Total steps walked:

Notes

HOLME FELL

317 M (1040 FT)

REGION: Southern   OS GRID: NY315006

Date:

Companion:

Weather condition:

Descent start time:

Descent duration

Finish time:

Difficulty:

☆ ☆ ☆ ☆ ☆

Views

☆ ☆ ☆ ☆ ☆

Ascent start time:

Ascent duration:

Peak time:

Rating

☆ ☆ ☆ ☆ ☆

Total Duration:

Total distance:

Total steps walked:

Notes

....
....
....
....
....
....
....

BLACK FELL
323 M (1060 FT)

REGION: Southern OS GRID: NY340015

Date:

Companion:

Weather condition:

Descent start time:

Descent duration

Finish time:

Difficulty:

☆ ☆ ☆ ☆ ☆

Views

☆ ☆ ☆ ☆ ☆

Ascent start time:

Ascent duration:

Peak time:

Rating

☆ ☆ ☆ ☆ ☆

Total Duration:

Total distance:

Total steps walked:

Notes

....
....
....
....
....
....
....

LOUGHRIGG FELL

335 M (1099 FT)

REGION: Central   OS GRID: NY346051

Date:

Companion:

Descent start time:

Descent duration

Finish time:

Ascent start time:

Ascent duration:

Peak time:

Total Duration:

Total distance:

Total steps walked:

Weather condition:

Difficulty:

☆ ☆ ☆ ☆ ☆

Views

☆ ☆ ☆ ☆ ☆

Rating

☆ ☆ ☆ ☆ ☆

Notes

....
....
....
....
....
....
....

RANNERDALE KNOTTS

355 M (1165 FT)

REGION: North Western OS GRID: NY167182

Date:

Companion:

Weather condition:

Descent start time:

Descent duration

Finish time:

Difficulty:

☆ ☆ ☆ ☆

Views

Ascent start time:

Ascent duration:

Peak time:

☆ ☆ ☆ ☆

Rating

☆ ☆ ☆ ☆

Total Duration:

Total distance:

Total steps walked:

Notes

HIGH RIGG

357 M (1171 FT)

REGION: Central   OS GRID: NY308219

Date:

Companion:

Weather condition:

Descent start time:

Descent duration

Finish time:

Difficulty:

☆ ☆ ☆ ☆ ☆

Views

☆ ☆ ☆ ☆ ☆

Ascent start time:

Ascent duration:

Peak time:

Rating

☆ ☆ ☆ ☆ ☆

Total Duration:

Total distance:

Total steps walked:

Notes

....
....
....
....
....
....
....

SALE FELL
359 M (1178 FT)

REGION: North Western OS GRID: NY194296

Date:

Companion:

Weather condition:

Descent start time:

Descent duration

Finish time:

Difficulty:

☆ ☆ ☆ ☆ ☆

Views

Ascent start time:

Ascent duration:

Peak time:

☆ ☆ ☆ ☆ ☆

Rating

☆ ☆ ☆ ☆ ☆

Total Duration:

Total distance:

Total steps walked:

Notes

....
....
....
....
....
....
....

TROUTBECK TONGUE
364 M (1194 FT)

REGION: Far Eastern   OS GRID: NY422064

Date:

Companion:

Weather condition:

Descent start time:

Descent duration

Finish time:

Difficulty:

☆ ☆ ☆ ☆ ☆

Views

Ascent start time:

Ascent duration:

Peak time:

☆ ☆ ☆ ☆ ☆

Rating

☆ ☆ ☆ ☆ ☆

Total Duration:

Total distance:

Total steps walked:

Notes

LATRIGG

364 M (1194 FT)

REGION: Far Eastern   OS GRID: NY422064

Date: _____

Companion: _____

Weather condition:

☀️ ❄️ ⛈️ 🌧️ ⛅

Descent start time:

Descent duration

Finish time:

Difficulty:
☆ ☆ ☆ ☆ ☆

Views
☆ ☆ ☆ ☆ ☆

Ascent start time:

Ascent duration:

Peak time:

Rating
☆ ☆ ☆ ☆ ☆

Total Duration:

Total distance:

Total steps walked:

Notes

....
....
....
....
....
....
....

LING FELL
373 M (1224 FT)

REGION: Far Eastern   OS GRID: NY179285

Date:

Companion:

Weather condition:

☀ ❄ ⛈ 🌧 ☁

Descent start time:

Descent duration

Finish time:

Difficulty:

☆ ☆ ☆ ☆ ☆

Views

☆ ☆ ☆ ☆ ☆

Ascent start time:

Ascent duration:

Peak time:

Rating

☆ ☆ ☆ ☆ ☆

Total Duration:

Total distance:

Total steps walked:

Notes

....
....
....
....
....
....
....

WALLA CRAG
279 M (1243 FT)

REGION: Central

OS GRID: NY 276212

Date:

Companion:

Weather condition:

Descent start time:

Descent duration

Finish time:

Difficulty:

☆ ☆ ☆ ☆ ☆

Views

☆ ☆ ☆ ☆ ☆

Ascent start time:

Ascent duration:

Peak time:

Rating

☆ ☆ ☆ ☆ ☆

Total Duration:

Total distance:

Total steps walked:

Notes
....
....
....
....
....
....
....

HALLIN FELL
388 M (1273 FT)

REGION: Far Eastern				OS GRID: NY433198

Date: _____

Companion: _____

Weather condition:

☀ ❄ ⛈ 🌧 ☁

Descent start time:

Descent duration

Finish time:

Difficulty:
_____

☆ ☆ ☆ ☆ ☆

Views
_____

☆ ☆ ☆ ☆ ☆

Ascent start time:

Ascent duration:

Peak time:

Rating
_____

☆ ☆ ☆ ☆ ☆

Total Duration:

Total distance:

Total steps walked:

Notes
_____

....
....
....

....
....
....
....

15

SILVER HOW
395 M (1296 FT)

REGION: Central OS GRID: NY324066

Date:

Companion:

Descent start time:

Descent duration

Finish time:

Ascent start time:

Ascent duration:

Peak time:

Total Duration:

Total distance:

Total steps walked:

Weather condition:

Difficulty:

☆ ☆ ☆ ☆ ☆

Views

☆ ☆ ☆ ☆ ☆

Rating

☆ ☆ ☆ ☆ ☆

Notes

....
....
....
....
....
....
....

HELM CRAG

405 M (1329 FT)

REGION: Central   OS GRID: NY326093

Date:

Companion:

Weather condition:

Descent start time:

Descent duration

Finish time:

Difficulty:

☆ ☆ ☆ ☆ ☆

Views

☆ ☆ ☆ ☆ ☆

Ascent start time:

Ascent duration:

Peak time:

Rating

☆ ☆ ☆ ☆ ☆

Total Duration:

Total distance:

Total steps walked:

Notes

GRANGE FELL
416 M (1365 FT)

REGION: Western OS GRID: NY137226

Date:

Companion:

Weather condition:

Descent start time:

Descent duration

Finish time:

Difficulty:

☆ ☆ ☆ ☆ ☆

Views

☆ ☆ ☆ ☆ ☆

Ascent start time:

Ascent duration:

Peak time:

Rating

☆ ☆ ☆ ☆ ☆

Total Duration:

Total distance:

Total steps walked:

Notes

....
....
....
....
....
....
....

FELLBARROW

416 M (1365 FT)

REGION: Western   OS GRID: NY32242

Date:

Companion:

Descent start time:

Descent duration

Finish time:

Ascent start time:

Ascent duration:

Peak time:

Total Duration:

Total distance:

Total steps walked:

Weather condition:

Difficulty:

☆ ☆ ☆ ☆ ☆

Views

☆ ☆ ☆ ☆ ☆

Rating

☆ ☆ ☆ ☆ ☆

Notes

GIBSON KNOTT
420 M (1378 FT)

REGION: Central

OS GRID: NY316100

Date:

Companion:

Weather condition:

Descent start time:

Descent duration

Finish time:

Difficulty:

☆ ☆ ☆ ☆ ☆

Views

☆ ☆ ☆ ☆ ☆

Ascent start time:

Ascent duration:

Peak time:

Rating

☆ ☆ ☆ ☆ ☆

Total Duration:

Total distance:

Total steps walked:

Notes

....
....
....
....
....
....
....

BUCKBARROW

423 M (1388 FT)

REGION: Western

OS GRID: NY135061

Date:

Companion:

Weather condition:

Descent start time:

Descent duration

Finish time:

Difficulty:

☆ ☆ ☆ ☆ ☆

Views

Ascent start time:

Ascent duration:

Peak time:

☆ ☆ ☆ ☆ ☆

Rating

☆ ☆ ☆ ☆ ☆

Total Duration:

Total distance:

Total steps walked:

Notes

....
....
....
....
....
....
....

LOW FELL
423 M (1388 FT)

REGION: Western   OS GRID: NY137226

Date:

Companion:

Weather condition:

Descent start time:

Descent duration

Finish time:

Difficulty:

☆ ☆ ☆ ☆ ☆

Views

☆ ☆ ☆ ☆ ☆

Ascent start time:

Ascent duration:

Peak time:

Rating

☆ ☆ ☆ ☆ ☆

Total Duration:

Total distance:

Total steps walked:

Notes

STEEL KNOTTS
432 M (1417 FT)

REGION: Far Eastern OS GRID: NY440181

Date:

Companion:

Weather condition:

Descent start time:

Descent duration

Finish time:

Difficulty:

☆ ☆ ☆ ☆ ☆

Views

☆ ☆ ☆ ☆ ☆

Ascent start time:

Ascent duration:

Peak time:

Rating

☆ ☆ ☆ ☆ ☆

Total Duration:

Total distance:

Total steps walked:

Notes

ARNISON CRAG

433 M (1421 FT)

REGION: Eastern   OS GRID: NY393149

Date:

Companion:

Weather condition:

Descent start time:

Descent duration

Finish time:

Difficulty:

☆ ☆ ☆ ☆ ☆

Views

☆ ☆ ☆ ☆ ☆

Ascent start time:

Ascent duration:

Peak time:

Rating

☆ ☆ ☆ ☆ ☆

Total Duration:

Total distance:

Total steps walked:

Notes

....
....
....

....
....
....
....

GLENRIDDING DODD
442 M (1450 FT)

REGION: Eastern   OS GRID: NY380175

Date:

Companion:

Descent start time:

Descent duration

Finish time:

Ascent start time:

Ascent duration:

Peak time:

Total Duration:

Total distance:

Total steps walked:

Weather condition:

Difficulty:

☆ ☆ ☆ ☆ ☆

Views

☆ ☆ ☆ ☆ ☆

Rating

☆ ☆ ☆ ☆ ☆

Notes

BINSEY
447 M (1467 FT)

REGION: Northern   OS GRID: NY225355

Date:

Companion:

Weather condition:

Descent start time:

Descent duration

Finish time:

Difficulty:

☆ ☆ ☆ ☆ ☆

Views

☆ ☆ ☆ ☆ ☆

Ascent start time:

Ascent duration:

Peak time:

Rating

☆ ☆ ☆ ☆ ☆

Total Duration:

Total distance:

Total steps walked:

Notes

....
....
....
....
....
....
....

GREAT CRAG

449 M (1473 FT)

REGION: Central   OS GRID: NY270146

Date:

Companion:

Weather condition:

Descent start time:

Descent duration

Finish time:

Difficulty:

☆ ☆ ☆ ☆ ☆

Views

Ascent start time:

Ascent duration:

Peak time:

☆ ☆ ☆ ☆ ☆

Rating

☆ ☆ ☆ ☆ ☆

Total Duration:

Total distance:

Total steps walked:

Notes

NAB SCAR
450 M (1476 FT)

REGION: Eastern　　　　　　　　　OS GRID: NY355072

Date:

Companion:

Descent start time:

Descent duration

Finish time:

Ascent start time:

Ascent duration:

Peak time:

Total Duration:

Total distance:

Total steps walked:

Weather condition:

Difficulty:

☆ ☆ ☆ ☆ ☆

Views

☆ ☆ ☆ ☆ ☆

Rating

☆ ☆ ☆ ☆ ☆

Notes

CATBELLS
451 M (1480 FT)

REGION: North Western OS GRID: NY244198

Date:

Companion:

Descent start time:

Descent duration

Finish time:

Ascent start time:

Ascent duration:

Peak time:

Total Duration:

Total distance:

Total steps walked:

Weather condition:

Difficulty:

☆ ☆ ☆ ☆ ☆

Views

☆ ☆ ☆ ☆ ☆

Rating

☆ ☆ ☆ ☆ ☆

Notes

....
....
....
....
....
....
....

GRAYSTONES

452 M (1483 FT)

REGION: North Western　　　　　　　　OS GRID: NY176266

Date: _____

Companion: _____

Weather condition:

Descent start time:

Descent duration

Finish time:

Difficulty:

☆ ☆ ☆ ☆ ☆

Views

☆ ☆ ☆ ☆ ☆

Ascent start time:

Ascent duration:

Peak time:

Rating

☆ ☆ ☆ ☆ ☆

Total Duration:

Total distance:

Total steps walked:

Notes

....
....
....
....
....
....
....

BARROW
455 M (1493 FT)

REGION: North Western

OS GRID: NY227218

Date:

Companion:

Descent start time:

Descent duration

Finish time:

Ascent start time:

Ascent duration:

Peak time:

Total Duration:

Total distance:

Total steps walked:

Weather condition:

Difficulty:

☆ ☆ ☆ ☆ ☆

Views

☆ ☆ ☆ ☆ ☆

Rating

☆ ☆ ☆ ☆ ☆

Notes

....
....
....
....
....
....
....

RAVEN CRAG

461 M (1512 FT)

REGION: Central OS GRID: NY303187

Date:

Companion:

Weather condition:

Descent start time:

Descent duration

Finish time:

Difficulty:

☆ ☆ ☆ ☆ ☆

Views

☆ ☆ ☆ ☆ ☆

Ascent start time:

Ascent duration:

Peak time:

Rating

☆ ☆ ☆ ☆ ☆

Total Duration:

Total distance:

Total steps walked:

Notes

....

....

....

....

....

....

....

◦ LINGMOOR FELL ◦
470 M (1542 FT)

REGION: Southern					OS GRID: NY302046

- Date:
- Companion:

Weather condition:

Descent start time:
Descent duration
Finish time:

Difficulty:

☆ ☆ ☆ ☆ ☆

Views

☆ ☆ ☆ ☆ ☆

Ascent start time:
Ascent duration:
Peak time:

Rating

☆ ☆ ☆ ☆ ☆

Total Duration:
Total distance:
Total steps walked:

Notes

ARMBOTH FELL
475 M (1558 FT)

REGION: Central OS GRID: NY295157

Date:

Companion:

Descent start time:

Descent duration

Finish time:

Ascent start time:

Ascent duration:

Peak time:

Total Duration:

Total distance:

Total steps walked:

Weather condition:

Difficulty:

☆ ☆ ☆ ☆ ☆

Views

☆ ☆ ☆ ☆ ☆

Rating

☆ ☆ ☆ ☆ ☆

Notes

BURNBANK FELL
475 M (1558 FT)

REGION: Southern OS GRID: NY302046

Date:

Companion:

Descent start time:

Descent duration

Finish time:

Ascent start time:

Ascent duration

Peak time:

Total Duration:

Total distance:

Total steps walked:

Weather condition:

Difficulty:

☆ ☆ ☆ ☆ ☆

Views

☆ ☆ ☆ ☆ ☆

Rating

☆ ☆ ☆ ☆ ☆

Notes

GOWBARROW FELL

481 M (1576 FT)

REGION: Eastern   OS GRID: NY407218

Date:

Companion:

Weather condition:

Descent start time:

Descent duration

Finish time:

Difficulty:

☆ ☆ ☆ ☆ ☆

Views

☆ ☆ ☆ ☆ ☆

Ascent start time:

Ascent duration:

Peak time:

Rating

☆ ☆ ☆ ☆ ☆

Total Duration:

Total distance:

Total steps walked:

Notes

SOUR HOWES
483 M (1585 FT)

REGION: Far Eastern

OS GRID: NY427032

Date:

Companion:

Weather condition:

Descent start time:

Descent duration

Finish time:

Difficulty:

☆ ☆ ☆ ☆ ☆

Views

☆ ☆ ☆ ☆ ☆

Ascent start time:

Ascent duration:

Peak time:

Rating

☆ ☆ ☆ ☆ ☆

Total Duration:

Total distance:

Total steps walked:

Notes

LONGLANDS FELL

483 M (1585 FT)

REGION: Nothern   OS GRID: NY275354

Date:

Companion:

Weather condition:

Descent start time:

Descent duration

Finish time:

Difficulty:

☆ ☆ ☆ ☆ ☆

Views

☆ ☆ ☆ ☆ ☆

Ascent start time:

Ascent duration:

Peak time:

Rating

☆ ☆ ☆ ☆ ☆

Total Duration:

Total distance:

Total steps walked:

Notes

....
....
....
....
....
....
....

BAYSTONES
487 M (1597 FT)

REGION: Far Eastern   OS GRID: NY403051

Date:

Companion:

Weather condition:

Descent start time:

Descent duration

Finish time:

Difficulty:

☆ ☆ ☆ ☆ ☆

Views

☆ ☆ ☆ ☆ ☆

Ascent start time:

Ascent duration:

Peak time:

Rating

☆ ☆ ☆ ☆ ☆

Total Duration:

Total distance:

Total steps walked:

Notes

GRIKE
488 M (1601 FT)

REGION: Western   OS GRID: NY084140

Date:

Companion:

Weather condition:

Descent start time:

Descent duration

Finish time:

Difficulty:

☆ ☆ ☆ ☆ ☆

Views

☆ ☆ ☆ ☆ ☆

Ascent start time:

Ascent duration:

Peak time:

Rating

☆ ☆ ☆ ☆ ☆

Total Duration:

Total distance:

Total steps walked:

Notes

....
....
....
....
....
....
....

GREEN CRAG

489 M (1603 FT)

REGION: Southern   OS GRID: SD200982

Date:

Companion:

Weather condition:

Descent start time:

Descent duration

Finish time:

Difficulty:

☆ ☆ ☆ ☆ ☆

Views

☆ ☆ ☆ ☆ ☆

Ascent start time:

Ascent duration:

Peak time:

Rating

☆ ☆ ☆ ☆ ☆

Total Duration:

Total distance:

Total steps walked:

Notes

....
....
....
....
....
....
....

DODD

502 M (1647 FT)

REGION: Northern   OS GRID: NY244273

Date:

Companion:

Weather condition:

Descent start time:

Descent duration

Finish time:

Difficulty:

☆ ☆ ☆ ☆ ☆

Views

☆ ☆ ☆ ☆ ☆

Ascent start time:

Ascent duration:

Peak time:

Rating

☆ ☆ ☆ ☆ ☆

Total Duration:

Total distance:

Total steps walked:

Notes

STONE ARTHUR
504 M (1654 FT)

REGION: Eastern OS GRID: NY347092

Date: _____

Companion: _____

Weather condition:
☀ ❄ ☁ 🌧 ☁

Descent start time:

Descent duration

Finish time:

Difficulty:
☆ ☆ ☆ ☆ ☆

Views
☆ ☆ ☆ ☆ ☆

Ascent start time:

Ascent duration:

Peak time:

Rating
☆ ☆ ☆ ☆ ☆

Total Duration:

Total distance:

Total steps walked:

Notes
....
....
....
....
....
....
....

LITTLE MELL FELL
505 M (1657 FT)

REGION: Eastern

OS GRID: NY423240

Date:

Companion:

Weather condition:

Descent start time:

Descent duration

Finish time:

Difficulty:

☆ ☆ ☆ ☆ ☆

Views

☆ ☆ ☆ ☆ ☆

Ascent start time:

Ascent duration:

Peak time:

Rating

☆ ☆ ☆ ☆ ☆

Total Duration:

Total distance:

Total steps walked:

Notes

....
....
....
....
....
....
....

LOW PIKE
508 M (1667 FT)

REGION: Eastern OS GRID: NY272078

Date: _____

Companion: _____

Descent start time:

Descent duration

Finish time:

Ascent start time:

Ascent duration:

Peak time:

Total Duration:

Total distance:

Total steps walked:

Weather condition:

☼ ❄ ⛈ 🌧 ☁

Difficulty:
☆ ☆ ☆ ☆ ☆

Views
☆ ☆ ☆ ☆ ☆

Rating
☆ ☆ ☆ ☆ ☆

Notes

....
....
....
....
....
....
....

BEDA FELL

509 M (1670 FT)

REGION: Far Eastern   OS GRID: NY428171

Date:

Companion:

Weather condition:

Descent start time:

Descent duration

Finish time:

Difficulty:

☆ ☆ ☆ ☆ ☆

Views

☆ ☆ ☆ ☆ ☆

Ascent start time:

Ascent duration:

Peak time:

Rating

☆ ☆ ☆ ☆ ☆

Total Duration:

Total distance:

Total steps walked:

Notes

....
....
....
....
....
....
....

HEN COMB
509 M (1670 FT)

REGION: Western OS GRID: NY132181

Date:

Companion:

Weather condition:

Descent start time:

Descent duration

Finish time:

Difficulty:

☆ ☆ ☆ ☆ ☆

Views

☆ ☆ ☆ ☆ ☆

Ascent start time:

Ascent duration:

Peak time:

Rating

☆ ☆ ☆ ☆ ☆

Total Duration:

Total distance:

Total steps walked:

Notes

....
....
....
....
....
....
....

47

BROOM FELL
511 M (1677 FT)

REGION: North Western   OS GRID: NY194271

Date: _____

Companion: _____

Weather condition:
☀ ❄ ☁ 🌧 ☁

Descent start time:

Descent duration

Finish time:

Difficulty:
☆ ☆ ☆ ☆ ☆

Views
☆ ☆ ☆ ☆ ☆

Ascent start time:

Ascent duration:

Peak time:

Rating
☆ ☆ ☆ ☆ ☆

Total Duration:

Total distance:

Total steps walked:

Notes
....
....
....
....
....
....
....

MELLBREAK
512 M (1680 FT)

REGION: Western   OS GRID: NY148186

Date: _____

Companion: _____

Weather condition:

Descent start time:

Descent duration

Finish time:

Difficulty:

☆ ☆ ☆ ☆ ☆

Views

☆ ☆ ☆ ☆ ☆

Ascent start time:

Ascent duration:

Peak time:

Rating

☆ ☆ ☆ ☆ ☆

Total Duration:

Total distance:

Total steps walked:

Notes

....
....
....
....
....
....
....

HIGH TOVE
515 M (1690 FT)

REGION: Central   OS GRID: NY289165

Date:

Companion:

Weather condition:

Descent start time:

Descent duration

Finish time:

Difficulty:

☆ ☆ ☆ ☆ ☆

Views

☆ ☆ ☆ ☆ ☆

Ascent start time:

Ascent duration:

Peak time:

Rating

☆ ☆ ☆ ☆ ☆

Total Duration:

Total distance:

Total steps walked:

Notes

....
....
....

....
....
....
....

SALLOWS
516 M (1693 FT)

REGION: Far Eastern OS GRID: NY436039

Date: _____

Companion: _____

Weather condition:

Descent start time:

Descent duration

Finish time:

Difficulty:

☆ ☆ ☆ ☆ ☆

Views

Ascent start time:

Ascent duration:

Peak time:

☆ ☆ ☆ ☆ ☆

Rating

☆ ☆ ☆ ☆ ☆

Total Duration:

Total distance:

Total steps walked:

Notes

....
....
....
....
....
....
....

WHINLATER

517 M (1696 FT)

REGION: Eastern OS GRID: NY191251

Date: _____

Companion: _____

Weather condition:

Descent start time:

Descent duration

Finish time:

Difficulty:
_____
☆ ☆ ☆ ☆ ☆

Views
_____
☆ ☆ ☆ ☆ ☆

Ascent start time:

Ascent duration:

Peak time:

Rating
_____
☆ ☆ ☆ ☆ ☆

Total Duration:

Total distance:

Total steps walked:

Notes
_____
....
....
....

....
....
....
....

HIGH HARTSTOP DODD
519 M (1703 FT)

REGION: Eastern OS GRID: NY393107

Date:

Companion:

Descent start time:

Descent duration

Finish time:

Ascent start time:

Ascent duration:

Peak time:

Total Duration:

Total distance:

Total steps walked:

Weather condition:

Difficulty:
☆ ☆ ☆ ☆ ☆

Views
☆ ☆ ☆ ☆ ☆

Rating
☆ ☆ ☆ ☆ ☆

Notes

....
....
....
....
....
....
....

SOUTHER FELL
522 M (1713 FT)

REGION: Northern OS GRID: NY354291

Date:

Companion:

Weather condition:

Descent start time:

Descent duration

Finish time:

Difficulty:

☆ ☆ ☆ ☆ ☆

Views

☆ ☆ ☆ ☆ ☆

Ascent start time:

Ascent duration:

Peak time:

Rating

☆ ☆ ☆ ☆ ☆

Total Duration:

Total distance:

Total steps walked:

Notes

CRAG FELL
523 M (1716 FT)

REGION: Western

OS GRID: NY097143

Date:

Companion:

Weather condition:

Descent start time:

Descent duration

Finish time:

Difficulty:

☆ ☆ ☆ ☆ ☆

Views

☆ ☆ ☆ ☆ ☆

Ascent start time:

Ascent duration:

Peak time:

Rating

☆ ☆ ☆ ☆ ☆

Total Duration:

Total distance:

Total steps walked:

Notes

....
....
....

....
....
....
....

BONSCALE PIKE
524 M (1719 FT)

REGION: Far Eastern OS GRID: NY453200

Date:

Companion:

Weather condition:

Descent start time:

Descent duration

Finish time:

Difficulty:

☆ ☆ ☆ ☆ ☆

Views

☆ ☆ ☆ ☆ ☆

Ascent start time:

Ascent duration:

Peak time:

Rating

☆ ☆ ☆ ☆ ☆

Total Duration:

Total distance:

Total steps walked:

Notes

EAGLE CRAG

525 M (1722 FT)

REGION: Central OS GRID: NY275121

Date:

Companion:

Weather condition:

Descent start time:

Descent duration

Finish time:

Difficulty:

☆ ☆ ☆ ☆ ☆

Views

☆ ☆ ☆ ☆ ☆

Ascent start time:

Ascent duration:

Peak time:

Rating

☆ ☆ ☆ ☆ ☆

Total Duration:

Total distance:

Total steps walked:

Notes

....
....
....

....
....
....
....

GAVEL FELL
526 M (1726 FT)

REGION: Western

OS GRID: NY116183

Date:

Companion:

Weather condition:

Descent start time:

Descent duration

Finish time:

Difficulty:

☆ ☆ ☆ ☆ ☆

Views

☆ ☆ ☆ ☆ ☆

Ascent start time:

Ascent duration:

Peak time:

Rating

☆ ☆ ☆ ☆ ☆

Total Duration:

Total distance:

Total steps walked:

Notes

GREAT COCKUP
526 M (1726 FT)

REGION: Northern

OS GRID: NY273333

Date: _____

Companion: _____

Weather condition:

☀ ❄ ⛈ 🌧 ☁

Descent start time:

Descent duration

Finish time:

Difficulty:

☆ ☆ ☆ ☆ ☆

Views

☆ ☆ ☆ ☆ ☆

Ascent start time:

Ascent duration:

Peak time:

Rating

☆ ☆ ☆ ☆ ☆

Total Duration:

Total distance:

Total steps walked:

Notes

....
....
....
....
....
....
....

ARTHUR'S PIKE

533 M (1749 FT)

REGION: Far Eastern OS GRID: NY460206

Date:

Companion:

Weather condition:

Descent start time:

Descent duration

Finish time:

Difficulty:

☆ ☆ ☆ ☆ ☆

Views

☆ ☆ ☆ ☆ ☆

Ascent start time:

Ascent duration:

Peak time:

Rating

☆ ☆ ☆ ☆ ☆

Total Duration:

Total distance:

Total steps walked:

Notes

GREAT MELL FELL
537 M (1762 FT)

REGION: Eastern OS GRID: NY396253

Date:

Companion:

Weather condition:

Descent start time:

Descent duration

Finish time:

Difficulty:

☆ ☆ ☆ ☆ ☆

Views

☆ ☆ ☆ ☆ ☆

Ascent start time:

Ascent duration:

Peak time:

Rating

☆ ☆ ☆ ☆ ☆

Total Duration:

Total distance:

Total steps walked:

Notes

....
....
....

....
....
....
....

WHIN RIGG
537 M (1762 FT)

REGION: Southern

OS GRID: NY151035

Date:

Companion:

Weather condition:

Descent start time:

Descent duration

Finish time:

Difficulty:

☆ ☆ ☆ ☆ ☆

Views

☆ ☆ ☆ ☆ ☆

Ascent start time:

Ascent duration:

Peak time:

Rating

☆ ☆ ☆ ☆ ☆

Total Duration:

Total distance:

Total steps walked:

Notes

CALF CRAG
537 M (1762 FT)

REGION: Central OS GRID: NY301104

Date:

Companion:

Weather condition:

Descent start time:

Descent duration

Finish time:

Difficulty:

☆ ☆ ☆ ☆ ☆

Views

☆ ☆ ☆ ☆ ☆

Ascent start time:

Ascent duration:

Peak time:

Rating

☆ ☆ ☆ ☆ ☆

Total Duration:

Total distance:

Total steps walked:

Notes

....
....
....

....
....
....
....

LANK RIGG
541 M (1775 FT)

REGION: Western

OS GRID: NY091119

Date:

Companion:

Weather condition:

Descent start time:

Descent duration

Finish time:

Difficulty:

☆ ☆ ☆ ☆ ☆

Views

Ascent start time:

Ascent duration:

Peak time:

☆ ☆ ☆ ☆ ☆

Rating

☆ ☆ ☆ ☆ ☆

Total Duration:

Total distance:

Total steps walked:

Notes

....
....
....

....
....
....
....

BLEA RIGG
541 M (1775 FT)

REGION: Western OS GRID: NY091119

Date: _____

Companion: _____

Weather condition:

Descent start time:

Descent duration

Finish time:

Difficulty:

☆ ☆ ☆ ☆ ☆

Views

☆ ☆ ☆ ☆ ☆

Ascent start time:

Ascent duration:

Peak time:

Rating

☆ ☆ ☆ ☆ ☆

Total Duration:

Total distance:

Total steps walked:

Notes

....
....
....
....
....
....
....

HARD KNOTT
549 M (1801 FT)

REGION: Southern

OS GRID: NY231023

Date:

Companion:

Weather condition:

Descent start time:

Descent duration

Finish time:

Difficulty:

☆ ☆ ☆ ☆ ☆

Views

☆ ☆ ☆ ☆ ☆

Ascent start time:

Ascent duration:

Peak time:

Rating

☆ ☆ ☆ ☆ ☆

Total Duration:

Total distance:

Total steps walked:

Notes

....
....
....
....
....
....
....

TARN CRAG
549 M (1801 FT)

REGION: Central

OS GRID: NY303093

Date:

Companion:

Weather condition:

Descent start time:

Descent duration

Finish time:

Difficulty:

☆ ☆ ☆ ☆ ☆

Views

☆ ☆ ☆ ☆ ☆

Ascent start time:

Ascent duration:

Peak time:

Rating

☆ ☆ ☆ ☆ ☆

Total Duration:

Total distance:

Total steps walked:

Notes

MEAL FELL

550 M (1804 FT)

REGION: Northern

OS GRID: NY283337

Date:

Companion:

Weather condition:

Descent start time:

Descent duration

Finish time:

Difficulty:

☆ ☆ ☆ ☆ ☆

Views

Ascent start time:

Ascent duration:

Peak time:

☆ ☆ ☆ ☆ ☆

Rating

☆ ☆ ☆ ☆ ☆

Total Duration:

Total distance:

Total steps walked:

Notes

....
....
....
....
....
....
....

ROSTHWAITE FELL

551 M (1808 FT)

REGION: Southern   OS GRID: NY258124

Date:

Companion:

Descent start time:

Descent duration

Finish time:

Ascent start time:

Ascent duration:

Peak time:

Total Duration:

Total distance:

Total steps walked:

Weather condition:

Difficulty:

☆ ☆ ☆ ☆ ☆

Views

☆ ☆ ☆ ☆ ☆

Rating

☆ ☆ ☆ ☆ ☆

Notes

....
....
....
....
....
....
....

LORD'S SEAT

552 M (1811 FT)

REGION: North Western OS GRID: NY204265

Date:

Companion:

Weather condition:

Descent start time:

Descent duration

Finish time:

Difficulty:

☆ ☆ ☆ ☆ ☆

Views

☆ ☆ ☆ ☆ ☆

Ascent start time:

Ascent duration:

Peak time:

Rating

☆ ☆ ☆ ☆ ☆

Total Duration:

Total distance:

Total steps walked:

Notes

STEEL FELL

553 M (1814 FT)

REGION: Central　　　　　　　　　　OS GRID: NY319111

Date:

Companion:

Weather condition:

Descent start time:

Descent duration

Finish time:

Difficulty:

☆ ☆ ☆ ☆ ☆

Views

☆ ☆ ☆ ☆ ☆

Ascent start time:

Ascent duration:

Peak time:

Rating

☆ ☆ ☆ ☆ ☆

Total Duration:

Total distance:

Total steps walked:

Notes

KNOTT RIGG
556 M (1824 FT)

REGION: Western

OS GRID: NY197188

Date:

Companion:

Weather condition:

Descent start time:

Descent duration

Finish time:

Difficulty:

☆ ☆ ☆ ☆ ☆

Views

☆ ☆ ☆ ☆ ☆

Ascent start time:

Ascent duration:

Peak time:

Rating

☆ ☆ ☆ ☆ ☆

Total Duration:

Total distance:

Total steps walked:

Notes

BROCK CRAGS
561 M (1841 FT)

REGION: Far Eastern

OS GRID: NY416136

Date:

Companion:

Weather condition:

Descent start time:

Descent duration

Finish time:

Difficulty:

☆ ☆ ☆ ☆ ☆

Views

☆ ☆ ☆ ☆ ☆

Ascent start time:

Ascent duration:

Peak time:

Rating

☆ ☆ ☆ ☆ ☆

Total Duration:

Total distance:

Total steps walked:

Notes

ANGLETARN PIKES

567 M (1860 FT)

REGION: Far Eastern   OS GRID: NY413148

Date: _____

Companion: _____

Weather condition:

☀ ❄ ⛈ 🌧 ☁

Descent start time:

Descent duration

Finish time:

Difficulty:
_____
☆ ☆ ☆ ☆ ☆

Views
_____
☆ ☆ ☆ ☆ ☆

Ascent start time:

Ascent duration:

Peak time:

Rating
_____
☆ ☆ ☆ ☆ ☆

Total Duration:

Total distance:

Total steps walked:

Notes
_____
....
....
....
....
....
....
....

OUTERSIDE

568 M (1864 FT)

REGION: North Western   OS GRID: NY211214

Date:

Companion:

Weather condition:

Descent start time:

Descent duration

Finish time:

Difficulty:

☆ ☆ ☆ ☆ ☆

Views

☆ ☆ ☆ ☆ ☆

Ascent start time:

Ascent duration:

Peak time:

Rating

☆ ☆ ☆ ☆ ☆

Total Duration:

Total distance:

Total steps walked:

Notes

....
....
....
....
....
....
....

SERGEANT'S CRAG

571 M (1873 FT)

REGION: Central   OS GRID: NY273113

Date:

Companion:

Weather condition:

Descent start time:

Descent duration

Finish time:

Difficulty:

☆ ☆ ☆ ☆ ☆

Views

☆ ☆ ☆ ☆ ☆

Ascent start time:

Ascent duration:

Peak time:

Rating

☆ ☆ ☆ ☆ ☆

Total Duration:

Total distance:

Total steps walked:

Notes

BLAKE FELL
573 M (1880 FT)

REGION: Western OS GRID: NY110196

Date:

Companion:

Weather condition:

Descent start time:

Descent duration

Finish time:

Difficulty:

☆ ☆ ☆ ☆ ☆

Views

☆ ☆ ☆ ☆ ☆

Ascent start time:

Ascent duration:

Peak time:

Rating

☆ ☆ ☆ ☆ ☆

Total Duration:

Total distance:

Total steps walked:

Notes

MAIDEN MOOR
575 M (1886 FT)

REGION: North Western OS GRID: NY236181

Date:

Companion:

Weather condition:

Descent start time:

Descent duration

Finish time:

Difficulty:

☆ ☆ ☆ ☆ ☆

Views

☆ ☆ ☆ ☆ ☆

Ascent start time:

Ascent duration:

Peak time:

Rating

☆ ☆ ☆ ☆ ☆

Total Duration:

Total distance:

Total steps walked:

Notes

THE NAB
576 M (1890 FT)

REGION: Far Eastern
OS GRID: NY434151

Date:

Companion:

Weather condition:

Descent start time:

Descent duration

Finish time:

Difficulty:

☆ ☆ ☆ ☆ ☆

Views

☆ ☆ ☆ ☆ ☆

Ascent start time:

Ascent duration:

Peak time:

Rating

☆ ☆ ☆ ☆ ☆

Total Duration:

Total distance:

Total steps walked:

Notes

HARTSTOP ABOVE HOW
581 M (1906 FT)

REGION: Eastern

OS GRID: NY383120

Date:

Companion:

Weather condition:

Descent start time:

Descent duration

Finish time:

Difficulty:

☆ ☆ ☆ ☆ ☆

Views

☆ ☆ ☆ ☆ ☆

Ascent start time:

Ascent duration:

Peak time:

Rating

☆ ☆ ☆ ☆ ☆

Total Duration:

Total distance:

Total steps walked:

Notes

ARD CRAG

581 M (1906 FT)

REGION: North Western OS GRID: NY206197

Date:

Companion:

Weather condition:

Descent start time:

Descent duration

Finish time:

Difficulty:

☆ ☆ ☆ ☆ ☆

Views

☆ ☆ ☆ ☆ ☆

Ascent start time:

Ascent duration:

Peak time:

Rating

☆ ☆ ☆ ☆ ☆

Total Duration:

Total distance:

Total steps walked:

Notes

MIDDLE FELL
582 M (1909 FT)

REGION: Western

OS GRID: NY150072

Date:

Companion:

Weather condition:

Descent start time:

Descent duration

Finish time:

Difficulty:

☆ ☆ ☆ ☆ ☆

Views

☆ ☆ ☆ ☆ ☆

Ascent start time:

Ascent duration:

Peak time:

Rating

☆ ☆ ☆ ☆ ☆

Total Duration:

Total distance:

Total steps walked:

Notes

....
....
....
....
....
....
....

BRAE FELL
586 M (1923 FT)

REGION: Northern OS GRID: NY288351

Date:

Companion:

Weather condition:

Descent start time:

Descent duration

Finish time:

Difficulty:

☆ ☆ ☆ ☆ ☆

Views

☆ ☆ ☆ ☆ ☆

Ascent start time:

Ascent duration:

Peak time:

Rating

☆ ☆ ☆ ☆ ☆

Total Duration:

Total distance:

Total steps walked:

Notes

....
....
....
....
....
....
....

SHIPMAN KNOTTS

587 M (1926 FT)

REGION: Far Eastern   OS GRID: NY472062

Date:

Companion:

Weather condition:

Descent start time:

Descent duration

Finish time:

Difficulty:

☆ ☆ ☆ ☆ ☆

Views

Ascent start time:

Ascent duration:

Peak time:

☆ ☆ ☆ ☆ ☆

Rating

☆ ☆ ☆ ☆ ☆

Total Duration:

Total distance:

Total steps walked:

Notes

....
....
....
....
....
....
....

BLEABERRY FELL
590 M (1936 FT)

REGION: Central

OS GRID: NY285195

Date:

Companion:

Weather condition:

Descent start time:

Descent duration

Finish time:

Difficulty:

☆ ☆ ☆ ☆ ☆

Views

☆ ☆ ☆ ☆ ☆

Ascent start time:

Ascent duration:

Peak time:

Rating

☆ ☆ ☆ ☆ ☆

Total Duration:

Total distance:

Total steps walked:

Notes

....
....
....

....
....
....
....

HAYSTACK'S
597 M (1955 FT)

REGION: Western   OS GRID: NY193131

Date:

Companion:

Weather condition:

☀ ❄ ☁⚡ 🌧 ☁

Descent start time:

Descent duration

Finish time:

Difficulty:

☆ ☆ ☆ ☆ ☆

Views

Ascent start time:

Ascent duration:

Peak time:

☆ ☆ ☆ ☆ ☆

Rating

☆ ☆ ☆ ☆ ☆

Total Duration:

Total distance:

Total steps walked:

Notes

SEATHWAITE FELL
601 M (1972 FT)

REGION: SouthernOS GRID: NY229101

Date:

Companion:

Weather condition:

Descent start time:

Descent duration

Finish time:

Difficulty:

☆ ☆ ☆ ☆ ☆

Views

Ascent start time:

Ascent duration:

Peak time:

☆ ☆ ☆ ☆ ☆

Rating

☆ ☆ ☆ ☆ ☆

Total Duration:

Total distance:

Total steps walked:

Notes

....
....
....
....
....
....
....

HIGH SEAT
608 M (1995 FT)

REGION: Central

OS GRID: NY287180

Date:

Companion:

Weather condition:

Descent start time:

Descent duration

Finish time:

Difficulty:

☆ ☆ ☆ ☆ ☆

Views

☆ ☆ ☆ ☆ ☆

Ascent start time:

Ascent duration:

Peak time:

Rating

☆ ☆ ☆ ☆ ☆

Total Duration:

Total distance:

Total steps walked:

Notes

ILLGILL HEAD

609 M (1998 FT)

REGION: Southern OS GRID: NY168049

Date:

Companion:

Weather condition:

Descent start time:

Descent duration

Finish time:

Difficulty:

☆ ☆ ☆ ☆ ☆

Views

☆ ☆ ☆ ☆ ☆

Ascent start time:

Ascent duration:

Peak time:

Rating

☆ ☆ ☆ ☆ ☆

Total Duration:

Total distance:

Total steps walked:

Notes

HERON PIKE
612 M (2008 FT)

REGION: Eastern

OS GRID: NY355083

Date:

Companion:

Weather condition:

Descent start time:

Descent duration

Finish time:

Difficulty:

☆ ☆ ☆ ☆ ☆

Views

☆ ☆ ☆ ☆ ☆

Ascent start time:

Ascent duration:

Peak time:

Rating

☆ ☆ ☆ ☆ ☆

Total Duration:

Total distance:

Total steps walked:

Notes

GREAT BORNE

616 M (2021 FT)

REGION: Western   OS GRID: NY123163

Date:

Companion:

Weather condition:

Descent start time:

Descent duration

Finish time:

Difficulty:

☆ ☆ ☆ ☆ ☆

Views

☆ ☆ ☆ ☆ ☆

Ascent start time:

Ascent duration:

Peak time:

Rating

☆ ☆ ☆ ☆ ☆

Total Duration:

Total distance:

Total steps walked:

Notes

....
....
....
....
....
....
....

HARTSTOP DODD
618 M (2028 FT)

REGION: Far Eastern

OS GRID: NY411118

Date:

Companion:

Weather condition:

Descent start time:

Descent duration

Finish time:

Difficulty:

☆ ☆ ☆ ☆ ☆

Views

☆ ☆ ☆ ☆ ☆

Ascent start time:

Ascent duration:

Peak time:

Rating

☆ ☆ ☆ ☆ ☆

Total Duration:

Total distance:

Total steps walked:

Notes

BIRKS
622 M (2041 FT)

REGION: Eastern

OS GRID: NY380143

Date:

Companion:

Weather condition:

Descent start time:

Descent duration

Finish time:

Difficulty:

☆ ☆ ☆ ☆ ☆

Views

☆ ☆ ☆ ☆ ☆

Ascent start time:

Ascent duration:

Peak time:

Rating

☆ ☆ ☆ ☆ ☆

Total Duration:

Total distance:

Total steps walked:

Notes

....
....
....

....
....
....
....

YEWBARROWS

627 M (2057 FT)

REGION: Western   OS GRID: NY173084

Date:

Companion:

Weather condition:

Descent start time:

Descent duration

Finish time:

Difficulty:

☆ ☆ ☆ ☆ ☆

Views

☆ ☆ ☆ ☆ ☆

Ascent start time:

Ascent duration:

Peak time:

Rating

☆ ☆ ☆ ☆ ☆

Total Duration:

Total distance:

Total steps walked:

Notes

....
....
....
....
....
....
....

MUNGRISDALE COMMON
633 M (2077 FT)

REGION: Northern   OS GRID: NY310292

Date:

Companion:

Weather condition:

Descent start time:

Descent duration

Finish time:

Difficulty:

☆ ☆ ☆ ☆ ☆

Views

☆ ☆ ☆ ☆ ☆

Ascent start time:

Ascent duration:

Peak time:

Rating

☆ ☆ ☆ ☆ ☆

Total Duration:

Total distance:

Total steps walked:

Notes

....
....
....
....
....
....
....

STARLING DODD

633 M (2077 FT)

REGION: Western

OS GRID: NY142157

Date:

Companion:

Weather condition:

Descent start time:

Descent duration

Finish time:

Difficulty:

☆ ☆ ☆ ☆ ☆

Views

☆ ☆ ☆ ☆ ☆

Ascent start time:

Ascent duration:

Peak time:

Rating

☆ ☆ ☆ ☆ ☆

Total Duration:

Total distance:

Total steps walked:

Notes

LITTLE HART CRAG

637 M (2090 FT)

REGION: Eastern

OS GRID: NY387100

Date:

Companion:

Weather condition:

Descent start time:

Descent duration

Finish time:

Difficulty:

☆ ☆ ☆ ☆ ☆

Views

☆ ☆ ☆ ☆ ☆

Ascent start time:

Ascent duration:

Peak time:

Rating

☆ ☆ ☆ ☆ ☆

Total Duration:

Total distance:

Total steps walked:

Notes

....
....
....
....
....
....
....

CAUSEY PIKE

637 M (2090 FT)

REGION: North Western   OS GRID: NY218208

Date:

Companion:

Weather condition:

Descent start time:

Descent duration

Finish time:

Difficulty:

☆ ☆ ☆ ☆ ☆

Views

☆ ☆ ☆ ☆ ☆

Ascent start time:

Ascent duration:

Peak time:

Rating

☆ ☆ ☆ ☆ ☆

Total Duration:

Total distance:

Total steps walked:

Notes

GREY CRAG
638 M (2093 FT)

REGION: Far Eastern

OS GRID: NY497072

Date:

Companion:

Weather condition:

Descent start time:

Descent duration

Finish time:

Difficulty:

☆ ☆ ☆ ☆ ☆

Views

☆ ☆ ☆ ☆ ☆

Ascent start time:

Ascent duration:

Peak time:

Rating

☆ ☆ ☆ ☆ ☆

Total Duration:

Total distance:

Total steps walked:

Notes

BASE BROWN
646 M (2119 FT)

REGION: Western

OS GRID: NY225114

Date:

Companion:

Weather condition:

Descent start time:

Descent duration

Finish time:

Difficulty:

☆ ☆ ☆ ☆ ☆

Views

☆ ☆ ☆ ☆ ☆

Ascent start time:

Ascent duration:

Peak time:

Rating

☆ ☆ ☆ ☆ ☆

Total Duration:

Total distance:

Total steps walked:

Notes

FLEETWITH PIKE

649 M (2129 FT)

REGION: Western

OS GRID: NY205141

Date:

Companion:

Weather condition:

☀ ❄ ⛈ 🌧 ☁

Descent start time:

Descent duration

Finish time:

Difficulty:

☆ ☆ ☆ ☆ ☆

Views

☆ ☆ ☆ ☆ ☆

Ascent start time:

Ascent duration:

Peak time:

Rating

☆ ☆ ☆ ☆ ☆

Total Duration:

Total distance:

Total steps walked:

Notes

....
....
....
....
....
....
....

ROSETT PIKE
651 M (2136 FT)

REGION: Southern

OS GRID: NY249075

Date: _____

Companion: _____

Weather condition:

☀ ❄ ⛈ 🌧 ☁

Descent start time:

Descent duration

Finish time:

Difficulty:
☆ ☆ ☆ ☆ ☆

Views
☆ ☆ ☆ ☆ ☆

Ascent start time:

Ascent duration:

Peak time:

Rating
☆ ☆ ☆ ☆ ☆

Total Duration:

Total distance:

Total steps walked:

Notes

GREAT SCAFELL

651M (2136 FT)

REGION: Nothern   OS GRID: NY291339

Date:

Companion:

Weather condition:

Descent start time:

Descent duration

Finish time:

Difficulty:

☆ ☆ ☆ ☆ ☆

Views

☆ ☆ ☆ ☆ ☆

Ascent start time:

Ascent duration:

Peak time:

Rating

☆ ☆ ☆ ☆ ☆

Total Duration:

Total distance:

Total steps walked:

Notes

HIGH SPY
658 M (2159 FT)

REGION: North Western

OS GRID: NY318350

Date: _____

Companion: _____

Weather condition:
☀ ❄ ⛈ 🌧 ☁

Descent start time:

Descent duration

Finish time:

Difficulty:
☆ ☆ ☆ ☆ ☆

Views
☆ ☆ ☆ ☆ ☆

Ascent start time:

Ascent duration:

Peak time:

Rating
☆ ☆ ☆ ☆ ☆

Total Duration:

Total distance:

Total steps walked:

Notes

....
....
....
....
....
....
....

HARTER FELL

654 M (2146 FT)

REGION: Southern   OS GRID: SD218997

Date:

Companion:

Descent start time:

Descent duration

Finish time:

Ascent start time:

Ascent duration:

Peak time:

Total Duration:

Total distance:

Total steps walked:

Weather condition:

Difficulty:

☆ ☆ ☆ ☆ ☆

Views

☆ ☆ ☆ ☆ ☆

Rating

☆ ☆ ☆ ☆ ☆

Notes

MIDDLE DODD

654 M (2146 FT)

REGION: Eastern OS GRID: NY397095

Date: _____

Companion: _____

Descent start time:

Descent duration

Finish time:

Ascent start time:

Ascent duration:

Peak time:

Total Duration:

Total distance:

Total steps walked:

Weather condition:

☀ ❄ ⛈ 🌧 ⛅

Difficulty:

☆ ☆ ☆ ☆ ☆

Views

☆ ☆ ☆ ☆ ☆

Rating

☆ ☆ ☆ ☆ ☆

Notes

....
....
....
....
....
....
....

SELSIDE PIKE
655 M (2149 FT)

REGION: Far Eastern OS GRID: NY490111

Date:

Companion:

Weather condition:

Descent start time:

Descent duration

Finish time:

Difficulty:

☆ ☆ ☆ ☆ ☆

Views

☆ ☆ ☆ ☆ ☆

Ascent start time:

Ascent duration:

Peak time:

Rating

☆ ☆ ☆ ☆ ☆

Total Duration:

Total distance:

Total steps walked:

Notes

SCANDALE
656 M (2152FT)

REGION: Eastern   OS GRID: NY374088

Date: _____

Companion: _____

Descent start time:

Descent duration

Finish time:

Ascent start time:

Ascent duration:

Peak time:

Total Duration:

Total distance:

Total steps walked:

Weather condition:

Difficulty:
☆ ☆ ☆ ☆ ☆

Views
☆ ☆ ☆ ☆ ☆

Rating
☆ ☆ ☆ ☆ ☆

Notes

....
....
....
....
....
....
....

PLACE FELL
657 M (2156 FT)

REGION: Far Eastern   OS GRID: NY405169

Date:

Companion:

Weather condition:

Descent start time:

Descent duration

Finish time:

Difficulty:

☆ ☆ ☆ ☆ ☆

Views

☆ ☆ ☆ ☆ ☆

Ascent start time:

Ascent duration:

Peak time:

Rating

☆ ☆ ☆ ☆ ☆

Total Duration:

Total distance:

Total steps walked:

Notes

....
....
....
....
....
....
....

HIGH PIKE
656 M (2152 FT)

REGION: Eastern   OS GRID: NY374088

Date:

Companion:

Descent start time:

Descent duration

Finish time:

Ascent start time:

Ascent duration:

Peak time:

Total Duration:

Total distance:

Total steps walked:

Weather condition:

Difficulty:

☆ ☆ ☆ ☆ ☆

Views

☆ ☆ ☆ ☆ ☆

Rating

☆ ☆ ☆ ☆ ☆

Notes

....
....
....

....
....
....
....

WHITELESS PIKE
660 M (2165 FT)

REGION: North Western OS GRID: NY180189

Date:

Companion:

Weather condition:

Descent start time:

Descent duration

Finish time:

Difficulty:

☆ ☆ ☆ ☆ ☆

Views

☆ ☆ ☆ ☆ ☆

Ascent start time:

Ascent duration:

Peak time:

Rating

☆ ☆ ☆ ☆ ☆

Total Duration:

Total distance:

Total steps walked:

Notes

....
....
....

....
....
....
....

CARROCK FELL

663 M (2175 FT)

REGION: Nothern   OS GRID: NY341336

Date:

Companion:

Weather condition:

Descent start time:

Descent duration

Finish time:

Difficulty:

☆ ☆ ☆ ☆ ☆

Views

☆ ☆ ☆ ☆ ☆

Ascent start time:

Ascent duration:

Peak time:

Rating

☆ ☆ ☆ ☆ ☆

Total Duration:

Total distance:

Total steps walked:

Notes

....
....
....
....
....
....
....

113

TARN CRAG

664 M (2178 FT)

REGION: Far Eastern   OS GRID: NY488078

Date:

Companion:

Weather condition:

Descent start time:

Descent duration

Finish time:

Difficulty:

☆ ☆ ☆ ☆ ☆

Views

☆ ☆ ☆ ☆ ☆

Ascent start time:

Ascent duration:

Peak time:

Rating

☆ ☆ ☆ ☆ ☆

Total Duration:

Total distance:

Total steps walked:

Notes

....
....
....
....
....
....
....

WETHER HILL

671 M (2201 FT)

REGION: Far Eastern   OS GRID: NY455167

Date:

Companion:

Weather condition:

Descent start time:

Descent duration

Finish time:

Difficulty:

☆ ☆ ☆ ☆ ☆

Views

Ascent start time:

Ascent duration:

Peak time:

☆ ☆ ☆ ☆ ☆

Rating

☆ ☆ ☆ ☆ ☆

Total Duration:

Total distance:

Total steps walked:

Notes

LOADPOT HILL
672 M (2205 FT)

REGION: Far Eastern OS GRID: NY456180

Date:

Companion:

Weather condition:

Descent start time:

Descent duration

Finish time:

Difficulty:

☆ ☆ ☆ ☆ ☆

Views

☆ ☆ ☆ ☆ ☆

Ascent start time:

Ascent duration:

Peak time:

Rating

☆ ☆ ☆ ☆ ☆

Total Duration:

Total distance:

Total steps walked:

Notes

....
....
....

....
....
....
....

SCAR CRAGS

672 M (2205 FT)

REGION: North Western   OS GRID: NY208206

Date:

Companion:

Weather condition:

Descent start time:

Descent duration

Finish time:

Difficulty:

☆ ☆ ☆ ☆ ☆

Views

☆ ☆ ☆ ☆ ☆

Ascent start time:

Ascent duration:

Peak time:

Rating

☆ ☆ ☆ ☆ ☆

Total Duration:

Total distance:

Total steps walked:

Notes

....
....
....
....
....
....
....

BAKESTALL
673 M (2208 FT)

REGION: Nothern   OS GRID: NY266308

Date:

Companion:

Weather condition:

Descent start time:

Descent duration

Finish time:

Difficulty:

☆ ☆ ☆ ☆ ☆

Views

☆ ☆ ☆ ☆ ☆

Ascent start time:

Ascent duration:

Peak time:

Rating

☆ ☆ ☆ ☆ ☆

Total Duration:

Total distance:

Total steps walked:

Notes

SHEFFIELD PIKE

675 M (2215 FT)

REGION: Eastern OS GRID: NY369181

Date:

Companion:

Descent start time:

Descent duration

Finish time:

Ascent start time:

Ascent duration:

Peak time:

Total Duration:

Total distance:

Total steps walked:

Weather condition:

Difficulty:

☆ ☆ ☆ ☆ ☆

Views

☆ ☆ ☆ ☆ ☆

Rating

☆ ☆ ☆ ☆ ☆

Notes

LOFT CRAG

680 M (2231 FT)

REGION: Central OS GRID: NY277071

Date: _____

Companion: _____

Weather condition:

☀ ❄ ⛈ 🌧 ☁

Descent start time:

Descent duration

Finish time:

Difficulty:
_____

☆ ☆ ☆ ☆ ☆

Views
_____

☆ ☆ ☆ ☆ ☆

Ascent start time:

Ascent duration:

Peak time:

Rating
_____

☆ ☆ ☆ ☆ ☆

Total Duration:

Total distance:

Total steps walked:

Notes
_____

....
....
....

....
....
....
....

BANNERDALE CRAGS
683 M (2241 FT)

REGION: Northern   OS GRID: NY335290

Date: _____

Companion: _____

Weather condition:
☀ ❄ ☁ 🌧 ☁

Descent start time:

Descent duration

Finish time:

Difficulty:
☆ ☆ ☆ ☆ ☆

Views
☆ ☆ ☆ ☆ ☆

Ascent start time:

Ascent duration:

Peak time:

Rating
☆ ☆ ☆ ☆ ☆

Total Duration:

Total distance:

Total steps walked:

Notes
....
....
....
....
....
....
....

GREAT CALVA
690 M (2264 FT)

REGION: Northern

OS GRID: NY290311

Date:

Companion:

Weather condition:

Descent start time:

Descent duration

Finish time:

Difficulty:

☆ ☆ ☆ ☆ ☆

Views

☆ ☆ ☆ ☆ ☆

Ascent start time:

Ascent duration:

Peak time:

Rating

☆ ☆ ☆ ☆ ☆

Total Duration:

Total distance:

Total steps walked:

Notes

....
....
....
....
....
....
....

ULLOCK PIKE
690 M (2264 FT)

REGION: Nothern   OS GRID: NY244287

Date:

Companion:

Weather condition:

Descent start time:

Descent duration

Finish time:

Difficulty:

☆ ☆ ☆ ☆ ☆

Views

☆ ☆ ☆ ☆ ☆

Ascent start time:

Ascent duration:

Peak time:

Rating

☆ ☆ ☆ ☆ ☆

Total Duration:

Total distance:

Total steps walked:

Notes

....
....
....
....
....
....
....

SEATALLAN
692 M (2270 FT)

REGION: Western

OS GRID: NY140084

Date:

Companion:

Weather condition:

Descent start time:

Descent duration

Finish time:

Difficulty:

☆ ☆ ☆ ☆ ☆

Views

☆ ☆ ☆ ☆ ☆

Ascent start time:

Ascent duration:

Peak time:

Rating

☆ ☆ ☆ ☆ ☆

Total Duration:

Total distance:

Total steps walked:

Notes

....
....
....
....
....
....
....

REST DODD

696 M (2283 FT)

REGION: Far Eastern OS GRID: NY432136

Date:

Companion:

Weather condition:

Descent start time:

Descent duration

Finish time:

Difficulty:

☆ ☆ ☆ ☆ ☆

Views

☆ ☆ ☆ ☆ ☆

Ascent start time:

Ascent duration:

Peak time:

Rating

☆ ☆ ☆ ☆ ☆

Total Duration:

Total distance:

Total steps walked:

Notes

CAW FELL
697 M (2287 FT)

REGION: Western

OS GRID: NY132109

Date:

Companion:

Weather condition:

Descent start time:

Descent duration

Finish time:

Difficulty:

☆ ☆ ☆ ☆ ☆

Views

☆ ☆ ☆ ☆ ☆

Ascent start time:

Ascent duration:

Peak time:

Rating

☆ ☆ ☆ ☆ ☆

Total Duration:

Total distance:

Total steps walked:

Notes

....
....
....
....
....
....
....

GREY KNOTTS
697 M (2287 FT)

REGION: Western						OS GRID: NY217125

Date:

Companion:

Weather condition:

Descent start time:

Descent duration

Finish time:

Difficulty:

☆ ☆ ☆ ☆ ☆

Views

☆ ☆ ☆ ☆ ☆

Ascent start time:

Ascent duration:

Peak time:

Rating

☆ ☆ ☆ ☆ ☆

Total Duration:

Total distance:

Total steps walked:

Notes

....
....
....
....
....
....
....

GRAY CRAG
699 M (2293 FT)

REGION: Far Eastern   OS GRID: NY427117

Date:

Companion:

Weather condition:

Descent start time:

Descent duration

Finish time:

Difficulty:

☆ ☆ ☆ ☆ ☆

Views

☆ ☆ ☆ ☆ ☆

Ascent start time:

Ascent duration:

Peak time:

Rating

☆ ☆ ☆ ☆ ☆

Total Duration:

Total distance:

Total steps walked:

Notes

PAVEY ARK

700 M (2297 FT)

REGION: Central   OS GRID: NY284079

Date:

Companion:

Weather condition:

Descent start time:

Descent duration

Finish time:

Difficulty:

☆ ☆ ☆ ☆ ☆

Views

Ascent start time:

Ascent duration:

Peak time:

☆ ☆ ☆ ☆ ☆

Rating

☆ ☆ ☆ ☆ ☆

Total Duration:

Total distance:

Total steps walked:

Notes

....
....
....
....
....
....
....

COLD PIKE
701 M (2300 FT)

REGION: Southern   OS GRID: NY262036

Date:

Companion:

Descent start time:

Descent duration

Finish time:

Ascent start time:

Ascent duration:

Peak time:

Total Duration:

Total distance:

Total steps walked:

Weather condition:

Difficulty:

☆ ☆ ☆ ☆ ☆

Views

☆ ☆ ☆ ☆ ☆

Rating

☆ ☆ ☆ ☆ ☆

Notes

BOWSCALE FELL

702 M (2303 FT)

REGION: Northern OS GRID: NY333305

Date:

Companion:

Weather condition:

Descent start time:

Descent duration

Finish time:

Difficulty:

☆ ☆ ☆ ☆ ☆

Views

☆ ☆ ☆ ☆ ☆

Ascent start time:

Ascent duration:

Peak time:

Rating

☆ ☆ ☆ ☆ ☆

Total Duration:

Total distance:

Total steps walked:

Notes

PIKE OF BLISCO
705 M (2313 FT)

REGION: Southen

OS GRID: NY271042

Date:

Companion:

Weather condition:

Descent start time:

Descent duration

Finish time:

Difficulty:

☆ ☆ ☆ ☆ ☆

Views

☆ ☆ ☆ ☆ ☆

Ascent start time:

Ascent duration:

Peak time:

Rating

☆ ☆ ☆ ☆ ☆

Total Duration:

Total distance:

Total steps walked:

Notes

YOKE
706 M (2216 FT)

REGION: Far Eastern   OS GRID: NY437067

Date:

Companion:

Descent start time:

Descent duration

Finish time:

Ascent start time:

Ascent duration:

Peak time:

Total Duration:

Total distance:

Total steps walked:

Weather condition:

Difficulty:

☆ ☆ ☆ ☆ ☆

Views

☆ ☆ ☆ ☆ ☆

Rating

☆ ☆ ☆ ☆ ☆

Notes

WHITESIDE
707 M (2320 FT)

REGION: North Western　　　　　OS GRID: NY170219

Date:

Companion:

Descent start time:

Descent duration

Finish time:

Ascent start time:

Ascent duration:

Peak time:

Total Duration:

Total distance:

Total steps walked:

Weather condition:

Difficulty:

☆ ☆ ☆ ☆ ☆

Views

☆ ☆ ☆ ☆ ☆

Rating

☆ ☆ ☆ ☆ ☆

Notes

PIKE OF STICKLE

709 M (2326 FT)

REGION: Central   OS GRID: NY273073

Date: _____

Companion: _____

Weather condition:

☀ ❄ ☁⚡ 🌧 ☁

Descent start time:

Descent duration

Finish time:

Difficulty:
☆ ☆ ☆ ☆ ☆

Views
☆ ☆ ☆ ☆ ☆

Ascent start time:

Ascent duration:

Peak time:

Rating
☆ ☆ ☆ ☆ ☆

Total Duration:

Total distance:

Total steps walked:

Notes

....
....
....
....
....
....
....

KNOTT

710 M (2329 FT)

REGION: Northern   OS GRID: NY296329

Date:

Companion:

Weather condition:

Descent start time:

Descent duration

Finish time:

Difficulty:

☆ ☆ ☆ ☆ ☆

Views

Ascent start time:

Ascent duration:

Peak time:

☆ ☆ ☆ ☆ ☆

Rating

☆ ☆ ☆ ☆ ☆

Total Duration:

Total distance:

Total steps walked:

Notes

....
....
....
....
....
....
....

BRANSTREE

713 M (2339 FT)

REGION: Far Eastern OS GRID: NY478099

Date:

Companion:

Weather condition:

Descent start time:

Descent duration

Finish time:

Difficulty:

Views

Ascent start time:

Ascent duration:

Peak time:

Rating

Total Duration:

Total distance:

Total steps walked:

Notes

BRANDRETH
715 M (2346 FT)

REGION: Western

OS GRID: NY214119

Date:

Companion:

Weather condition:

Descent start time:

Descent duration

Finish time:

Difficulty:

☆ ☆ ☆ ☆ ☆

Views

☆ ☆ ☆ ☆ ☆

Ascent start time:

Ascent duration:

Peak time:

Rating

☆ ☆ ☆ ☆ ☆

Total Duration:

Total distance:

Total steps walked:

Notes

LONSCALE FELL

715 M (2346 FT)

REGION: Nothern   OS GRID: NY285271

Date:

Companion:

Weather condition:

Descent start time:

Descent duration

Finish time:

Difficulty:

☆ ☆ ☆ ☆ ☆

Views

☆ ☆ ☆ ☆ ☆

Ascent start time:

Ascent duration:

Peak time:

Rating

☆ ☆ ☆ ☆ ☆

Total Duration:

Total distance:

Total steps walked:

Notes

BIRKHOUSE MOOR
718 M (2356 FT)

REGION: Eastern

OS GRID: NY363159

Date:

Companion:

Weather condition:

Descent start time:

Descent duration

Finish time:

Difficulty:

☆ ☆ ☆ ☆ ☆

Views

☆ ☆ ☆ ☆ ☆

Ascent start time:

Ascent duration:

Peak time:

Rating

☆ ☆ ☆ ☆ ☆

Total Duration:

Total distance:

Total steps walked:

Notes

FROSWICK
720 M (2362 FT)

REGION: Far Eastern OS GRID: NY435085

Date:

Companion:

Weather condition:

Descent start time:

Descent duration

Finish time:

Difficulty:

☆ ☆ ☆ ☆ ☆

Views

☆ ☆ ☆ ☆ ☆

Ascent start time:

Ascent duration:

Peak time:

Rating

☆ ☆ ☆ ☆ ☆

Total Duration:

Total distance:

Total steps walked:

Notes

....
....
....
....
....
....
....

THUNACAR KNOTT
723 M (2372 FT)

REGION: Central

OS GRID: NY279079

Date: _____

Companion: _____

Weather condition:
☀ ❄ ⛈ 🌧 ☁

Descent start time:

Descent duration

Finish time:

Difficulty:
☆ ☆ ☆ ☆ ☆

Views
☆ ☆ ☆ ☆ ☆

Ascent start time:

Ascent duration:

Peak time:

Rating
☆ ☆ ☆ ☆ ☆

Total Duration:

Total distance:

Total steps walked:

Notes

....
....
....
....
....
....
....

CLOUGH HEAD

726 M (2382 FT)

REGION: Eastern OS GRID: NY333225

Date:

Companion:

Weather condition:

Descent start time:

Descent duration

Finish time:

Difficulty:

☆ ☆ ☆ ☆ ☆

Views

☆ ☆ ☆ ☆ ☆

Ascent start time:

Ascent duration:

Peak time:

Rating

☆ ☆ ☆ ☆ ☆

Total Duration:

Total distance:

Total steps walked:

Notes

ULLSCARF

726 M (2382 FT)

REGION: Central

OS GRID: NY291121

Date:

Companion:

Weather condition:

Descent start time:

Descent duration

Finish time:

Difficulty:

☆ ☆ ☆ ☆ ☆

Views

☆ ☆ ☆ ☆ ☆

Ascent start time:

Ascent duration:

Peak time:

Rating

☆ ☆ ☆ ☆ ☆

Total Duration:

Total distance:

Total steps walked:

Notes

....
....
....
....
....
....
....

HINDSCARTH

727 M (2385 FT)

REGION: North Western   OS GRID: NY215165

Date:

Companion:

Weather condition:

☀ ❄ ⛈ 🌧 ☁

Descent start time:

Descent duration

Finish time:

Difficulty:

☆ ☆ ☆ ☆ ☆

Views

☆ ☆ ☆ ☆ ☆

Ascent start time:

Ascent duration:

Peak time:

Rating

☆ ☆ ☆ ☆ ☆

Total Duration:

Total distance:

Total steps walked:

Notes

KENTMERE PIKE

730 M (2395 FT)

REGION: Far Eastern   OS GRID: NY465077

Date:

Companion:

Weather condition:

Descent start time:

Descent duration

Finish time:

Difficulty:

☆ ☆ ☆ ☆ ☆

Views

☆ ☆ ☆ ☆ ☆

Ascent start time:

Ascent duration:

Peak time:

Rating

☆ ☆ ☆ ☆ ☆

Total Duration:

Total distance:

Total steps walked:

Notes

LONG SIDE
734 M (2408 FT)

REGION: Northern

OS GRID: NY248284

Date:

Companion:

Weather condition:

Descent start time:

Descent duration

Finish time:

Difficulty:

☆ ☆ ☆ ☆ ☆

Ascent start time:

Ascent duration:

Peak time:

Views

☆ ☆ ☆ ☆ ☆

Rating

☆ ☆ ☆ ☆ ☆

Total Duration:

Total distance:

Total steps walked:

Notes

....
....
....
....
....
....
....

SERGEANT MAN

736 M (2415 FT)

REGION: Eastern   OS GRID: NY286088

Date:

Companion:

Weather condition:

Descent start time:

Descent duration

Finish time:

Difficulty:

☆ ☆ ☆ ☆ ☆

Views

Ascent start time:

Ascent duration:

Peak time:

☆ ☆ ☆ ☆ ☆

Rating

☆ ☆ ☆ ☆ ☆

Total Duration:

Total distance:

Total steps walked:

Notes

HARRISON STICKLE

736 M (2415 FT)

REGION: Central   OS GRID: NY281074

Date:

Companion:

Weather condition:

Descent start time:

Descent duration

Finish time:

Difficulty:

☆ ☆ ☆ ☆ ☆

Views

Ascent start time:

Ascent duration:

Peak time:

☆ ☆ ☆ ☆ ☆

Rating

☆ ☆ ☆ ☆ ☆

Total Duration:

Total distance:

Total steps walked:

Notes

SEAT SANDAL

737 M (2417 FT)

REGION: Eastern OS GRID: NY344115

Date:

Companion:

Weather condition:

Descent start time:

Descent duration

Finish time:

Difficulty:

☆ ☆ ☆ ☆ ☆

Views

☆ ☆ ☆ ☆ ☆

Ascent start time:

Ascent duration:

Peak time:

Rating

☆ ☆ ☆ ☆ ☆

Total Duration:

Total distance:

Total steps walked:

Notes

....
....
....
....
....
....
....

ROBINSON
737 M (2418 FT)

REGION: North Western   OS GRID: NY201168

Date:

Companion:

Weather condition:

Descent start time:

Descent duration

Finish time:

Difficulty:

☆ ☆ ☆ ☆ ☆

Views

☆ ☆ ☆ ☆ ☆

Ascent start time:

Ascent duration:

Peak time:

Rating

☆ ☆ ☆ ☆ ☆

Total Duration:

Total distance:

Total steps walked:

Notes

THE KNOTT
739 M (2425 FT)

REGION: Far Eastern   OS GRID: NY132181

Date:

Companion:

Weather condition:

Descent start time:

Descent duration

Finish time:

Difficulty:

☆ ☆ ☆ ☆ ☆

Views

☆ ☆ ☆ ☆ ☆

Ascent start time:

Ascent duration:

Peak time:

Rating

☆ ☆ ☆ ☆ ☆

Total Duration:

Total distance:

Total steps walked:

Notes

....
....
....
....
....
....
....

HIGH CRAG
744 M (2441 FT)

REGION: Western OS GRID: NY180139

Date:

Companion:

Weather condition:

Descent start time:

Descent duration

Finish time:

Difficulty:

☆ ☆ ☆ ☆ ☆

Views

☆ ☆ ☆ ☆ ☆

Ascent start time:

Ascent duration:

Peak time:

Rating

☆ ☆ ☆ ☆ ☆

Total Duration:

Total distance:

Total steps walked:

Notes

....
....
....

....
....
....
....

CARL SIDE
746 M (2448 FT)

REGION: Northern   OS GRID: NY254280

Date:

Companion:

Weather condition:

Descent start time:

Descent duration

Finish time:

Difficulty:

☆ ☆ ☆ ☆ ☆

Views

Ascent start time:

Ascent duration:

Peak time:

☆ ☆ ☆ ☆ ☆

Rating

☆ ☆ ☆ ☆ ☆

Total Duration:

Total distance:

Total steps walked:

Notes

DALE HEAD
753 M (2470 FT)

REGION: North Western   OS GRID: NY222153

Date:

Companion:

Weather condition:

Descent start time:

Descent duration

Finish time:

Difficulty:

☆ ☆ ☆ ☆ ☆

Views

☆ ☆ ☆ ☆ ☆

Ascent start time:

Ascent duration:

Peak time:

Rating

☆ ☆ ☆ ☆ ☆

Total Duration:

Total distance:

Total steps walked:

Notes

....
....
....
....
....
....
....

RED PIKE
755 M (2477 FT)

REGION: Western

OS GRID: NY160154

Date:

Companion:

Weather condition:

Descent start time:

Descent duration

Finish time:

Difficulty:

☆ ☆ ☆ ☆ ☆

Views

☆ ☆ ☆ ☆ ☆

Ascent start time:

Ascent duration:

Peak time:

Rating

☆ ☆ ☆ ☆ ☆

Total Duration:

Total distance:

Total steps walked:

Notes

....
....
....

....
....
....
....

HART SIDE

756 M (2480 FT)

REGION: Eastern   OS GRID: NY359197

Date:

Companion:

Weather condition:

Descent start time:

Descent duration

Finish time:

Difficulty:

☆ ☆ ☆ ☆ ☆

Views

☆ ☆ ☆ ☆ ☆

Ascent start time:

Ascent duration:

Peak time:

Rating

☆ ☆ ☆ ☆ ☆

Total Duration:

Total distance:

Total steps walked:

Notes

ILL BELL
757 M (2484 FT)

REGION: Far Eastern OS GRID: NY436077

Date:

Companion:

Weather condition:

Descent start time:

Descent duration

Finish time:

Difficulty:

☆ ☆ ☆ ☆ ☆

Views

☆ ☆ ☆ ☆ ☆

Ascent start time:

Ascent duration:

Peak time:

Rating

☆ ☆ ☆ ☆ ☆

Total Duration:

Total distance:

Total steps walked:

Notes

....
....
....

....
....
....
....

MARDALE III BELL
760 M (2493 FT)

REGION: Far Eastern OS GRID: NY447101

Date:

Companion:

Weather condition:

Descent start time:

Descent duration

Finish time:

Difficulty:

☆ ☆ ☆ ☆ ☆

Views

☆ ☆ ☆ ☆ ☆

Ascent start time:

Ascent duration:

Peak time:

Rating

☆ ☆ ☆ ☆ ☆

Total Duration:

Total distance:

Total steps walked:

Notes

....
....
....
....
....
....
....

SLIGHT SIDE

762 M (2500 FT)

REGION: Southern OS GRID: NY209050

Date:

Companion:

Weather condition:

Descent start time:

Descent duration

Finish time:

Difficulty:

☆ ☆ ☆ ☆ ☆

Views

☆ ☆ ☆ ☆ ☆

Ascent start time:

Ascent duration:

Peak time:

Rating

☆ ☆ ☆ ☆ ☆

Total Duration:

Total distance:

Total steps walked:

Notes

HIGH RAISE

726 M (2500 FT)

REGION: Central　　　　　　　　OS GRID: NY280095

Date:

Companion:

Weather condition:

Descent start time:

Descent duration

Finish time:

Difficulty:

☆ ☆ ☆ ☆ ☆

Views

☆ ☆ ☆ ☆ ☆

Ascent start time:

Ascent duration:

Peak time:

Rating

☆ ☆ ☆ ☆ ☆

Total Duration:

Total distance:

Total steps walked:

Notes

....
....
....
....
....
....
....

WETHERLAM
763 M (2503 FT)

REGION: Southern　　　　　　　　OS GRID: NY288011

Date:

Companion:

Weather condition:

Descent start time:

Descent duration

Finish time:

Difficulty:

☆ ☆ ☆ ☆ ☆

Views

☆ ☆ ☆ ☆ ☆

Ascent start time:

Ascent duration:

Peak time:

Rating

☆ ☆ ☆ ☆ ☆

Total Duration:

Total distance:

Total steps walked:

Notes

....
....
....
....
....
....
....

STONY COVE PIKE
763 M (2503FT)

REGION: Far Eastern OS GRID: NY417100

Date: _____

Companion: _____

Weather condition:

☀ ❄ ⛈ 🌧 ⛅

Descent start time:

Descent duration

Finish time:

Difficulty:
☆ ☆ ☆ ☆ ☆

Views
☆ ☆ ☆ ☆ ☆

Ascent start time:

Ascent duration:

Peak time:

Rating
☆ ☆ ☆ ☆ ☆

Total Duration:

Total distance:

Total steps walked:

Notes

....
....
....
....
....
....
....

GREAT RIGG

766 M (2513 FT)

REGION: Eastern   OS GRID: NY355104

Date: _____

Companion: _____

Weather condition:

Descent start time:

Descent duration

Finish time:

Difficulty:
☆ ☆ ☆ ☆ ☆

Views
☆ ☆ ☆ ☆ ☆

Ascent start time:

Ascent duration:

Peak time:

Rating
☆ ☆ ☆ ☆ ☆

Total Duration:

Total distance:

Total steps walked:

Notes

HOPEGILL HEAD

770 M (2526 FT)

REGION: North Western OS GRID: NY185221

Date:

Companion:

Weather condition:

☀ ❄ ⛈ 🌧 ☁

Descent start time:

Descent duration

Finish time:

Difficulty:

☆ ☆ ☆ ☆ ☆

Views

☆ ☆ ☆ ☆ ☆

Ascent start time:

Ascent duration:

Peak time:

Rating

☆ ☆ ☆ ☆ ☆

Total Duration:

Total distance:

Total steps walked:

Notes

....
....
....
....
....
....
....

WANDOPE
772 M (2533 FT)

REGION: North Western   OS GRID: NY188197

Date:

Companion:

Weather condition:

Descent start time:

Descent duration

Finish time:

Difficulty:

☆ ☆ ☆ ☆ ☆

Views

☆ ☆ ☆ ☆ ☆

Ascent start time:

Ascent duration:

Peak time:

Rating

☆ ☆ ☆ ☆ ☆

Total Duration:

Total distance:

Total steps walked:

Notes

....
....
....
....
....
....
....

GREY FRAIR
773 M (2536 FT)

REGION: Southern

OS GRID: NY260003

Date:

Companion:

Weather condition:

Descent start time:

Descent duration

Finish time:

Difficulty:

☆ ☆ ☆ ☆ ☆

Views

☆ ☆ ☆ ☆ ☆

Ascent start time:

Ascent duration:

Peak time:

Rating

☆ ☆ ☆ ☆ ☆

Total Duration:

Total distance:

Total steps walked:

Notes

SAIL

773 M (2536 FT)

REGION: North Western   OS GRID: NY198202

Date:

Companion:

Weather condition:

Descent start time:

Descent duration

Finish time:

Difficulty:

☆ ☆ ☆ ☆ ☆

Views

☆ ☆ ☆ ☆ ☆

Ascent start time:

Ascent duration:

Peak time:

Rating

☆ ☆ ☆ ☆ ☆

Total Duration:

Total distance:

Total steps walked:

Notes

....
....
....
....
....
....
....

RED SCREES
776 M (2546 FT)

REGION: Eastern   OS GRID: NY396087

Date:

Companion:

Weather condition:

Descent start time:

Descent duration

Finish time:

Difficulty:

☆ ☆ ☆ ☆ ☆

Views

Ascent start time:

Ascent duration:

Peak time:

☆ ☆ ☆ ☆ ☆

Rating

☆ ☆ ☆ ☆ ☆

Total Duration:

Total distance:

Total steps walked:

Notes

....
....
....
....
....
....
....

DOW CRAG
778 M (2552 FT)

REGION: Southern   OS GRID: SD262977

Date: _____

Companion: _____

Weather condition:

Descent start time:

Descent duration

Finish time:

Difficulty:
☆ ☆ ☆ ☆ ☆

Views
☆ ☆ ☆ ☆ ☆

Ascent start time:

Ascent duration:

Peak time:

Rating
☆ ☆ ☆ ☆ ☆

Total Duration:

Total distance:

Total steps walked:

Notes
....
....
....
....
....
....
....

HARTER FELL
779 M (2556 FT)

REGION: Far Eastern OS GRID: NY459093

Date:

Companion:

Weather condition:

Descent start time:

Descent duration

Finish time:

Difficulty:

☆ ☆ ☆ ☆ ☆

Views

☆ ☆ ☆ ☆ ☆

Ascent start time:

Ascent duration:

Peak time:

Rating

☆ ☆ ☆ ☆ ☆

Total Duration:

Total distance:

Total steps walked:

Notes

....
....
....
....
....
....
....

KIDSTY PIKE
780 M (2559 FT)

REGION: Far Eastern OS GRID: NY447125

Date:

Companion:

Weather condition:

Descent start time:

Descent duration

Finish time:

Difficulty:

Views

Ascent start time:

Ascent duration:

Peak time:

Rating

Total Duration:

Total distance:

Total steps walked:

Notes

GLARAMARA

783 M (2569 FT)

REGION: Southern OS GRID: NY245104

Date:

Companion:

Weather condition:

Descent start time:

Descent duration

Finish time:

Difficulty:

☆ ☆ ☆ ☆ ☆

Views

☆ ☆ ☆ ☆ ☆

Ascent start time:

Ascent duration:

Peak time:

Rating

☆ ☆ ☆ ☆ ☆

Total Duration:

Total distance:

Total steps walked:

Notes

....
....
....
....
....
....
....

THORNTHWAITE CRAG
784 M (2572 FT)

REGION: Far Eastern   OS GRID: NY431100

Date:

Companion:

Weather condition:

Descent start time:

Descent duration

Finish time:

Difficulty:

☆ ☆ ☆ ☆ ☆

Views

☆ ☆ ☆ ☆ ☆

Ascent start time:

Ascent duration:

Peak time:

Rating

☆ ☆ ☆ ☆ ☆

Total Duration:

Total distance:

Total steps walked:

Notes

GREAT CARRS
785 M (2575 FT)

REGION: Southern   OS GRID: NY270009

Date:

Companion:

Weather condition:

Descent start time:

Descent duration

Finish time:

Difficulty:

☆ ☆ ☆ ☆ ☆

Views

Ascent start time:

Ascent duration:

Peak time:

☆ ☆ ☆ ☆ ☆

Rating

☆ ☆ ☆ ☆ ☆

Total Duration:

Total distance:

Total steps walked:

Notes

ALLEN CRAGS

785 M (2575 FT)

REGION: Southern OS GRID: NY236085

Date:

Companion:

Weather condition:

Descent start time:

Descent duration

Finish time:

Difficulty:

☆ ☆ ☆ ☆ ☆

Views

☆ ☆ ☆ ☆ ☆

Ascent start time:

Ascent duration:

Peak time:

Rating

☆ ☆ ☆ ☆ ☆

Total Duration:

Total distance:

Total steps walked:

Notes

....
....
....
....
....
....
....

WATSON'S DODD

789 M (2589 FT)

REGION: Eastern

OS GRID: NY335195

Date:

Companion:

Weather condition:

Descent start time:

Descent duration

Finish time:

Difficulty:

☆ ☆ ☆ ☆ ☆

Views

☆ ☆ ☆ ☆ ☆

Ascent start time:

Ascent duration:

Peak time:

Rating

☆ ☆ ☆ ☆ ☆

Total Duration:

Total distance:

Total steps walked:

Notes

....
....
....
....
....
....
....

GRISEDALE PIKE
791 M (2595 FT)

REGION: North Western OS GRID: NY198225

Date: _____

Companion: _____

Weather condition:

Descent start time:

Descent duration

Finish time:

Difficulty:

☆ ☆ ☆ ☆ ☆

Views

Ascent start time:

Ascent duration:

Peak time:

☆ ☆ ☆ ☆ ☆

Rating

☆ ☆ ☆ ☆ ☆

Total Duration:

Total distance:

Total steps walked:

Notes

....
....
....
....
....
....
....

DOVE CRAG

792 M (2598 FT)

REGION: Eastern OS GRID: NY374104

Date:

Companion:

Descent start time:

Descent duration

Finish time:

Ascent start time:

Ascent duration:

Peak time:

Total Duration:

Total distance:

Total steps walked:

Weather condition:

Difficulty:

☆ ☆ ☆ ☆ ☆

Views

☆ ☆ ☆ ☆ ☆

Rating

☆ ☆ ☆ ☆ ☆

Notes

RAMPSGILL HEAD
792 M (2598 FT)

REGION: Far Eastern

OS GRID: NY443128

Date:

Companion:

Weather condition:

Descent start time:

Descent duration

Finish time:

Difficulty:

☆ ☆ ☆ ☆ ☆

Views

☆ ☆ ☆ ☆ ☆

Ascent start time:

Ascent duration:

Peak time:

Rating

☆ ☆ ☆ ☆ ☆

Total Duration:

Total distance:

Total steps walked:

Notes

....
....
....

....
....
....
....

BRIM FELL
796 M (2612 FT)

REGION: Southern

OS GRID: SD270985

Date:

Companion:

Weather condition:

Descent start time:

Descent duration

Finish time:

Difficulty:

☆ ☆ ☆ ☆ ☆

Views

☆ ☆ ☆ ☆ ☆

Ascent start time:

Ascent duration:

Peak time:

Rating

☆ ☆ ☆ ☆ ☆

Total Duration:

Total distance:

Total steps walked:

Notes

HAYCOCK
797 M (2615 FT)

REGION: Western   OS GRID: NY144107

Date:

Companion:

Weather condition:

Descent start time:

Descent duration

Finish time:

Difficulty:

☆ ☆ ☆ ☆ ☆

Views

☆ ☆ ☆ ☆ ☆

Ascent start time:

Ascent duration:

Peak time:

Rating

☆ ☆ ☆ ☆ ☆

Total Duration:

Total distance:

Total steps walked:

Notes

....
....
....
....
....
....
....

GREEN GABLE

801 M (2595 FT)

REGION: Western   OS GRID: NY214107

Date:

Companion:

Weather condition:

Descent start time:

Descent duration

Finish time:

Difficulty:

☆ ☆ ☆ ☆ ☆

Views

☆ ☆ ☆ ☆ ☆

Ascent start time:

Ascent duration:

Peak time:

Rating

☆ ☆ ☆ ☆ ☆

Total Duration:

Total distance:

Total steps walked:

Notes

....
....
....
....
....
....
....

HIGH STREET
802 M (2631 FT)

REGION: Far Eastern
OS GRID: NY448137

Date:

Companion:

Weather condition:

Descent start time:

Descent duration

Finish time:

Difficulty:

☆ ☆ ☆ ☆ ☆

Views

Ascent start time:

Ascent duration:

Peak time:

☆ ☆ ☆ ☆ ☆

Rating

☆ ☆ ☆ ☆ ☆

Total Duration:

Total distance:

Total steps walked:

Notes

KIRK FELL
802 M (2631 FT)

REGION: Western

OS GRID: NY194104

Date:

Companion:

Weather condition:

Descent start time:

Descent duration

Finish time:

Difficulty:

☆ ☆ ☆ ☆ ☆

Views

☆ ☆ ☆ ☆ ☆

Ascent start time:

Ascent duration:

Peak time:

Rating

☆ ☆ ☆ ☆ ☆

Total Duration:

Total distance:

Total steps walked:

Notes

SWIRL HOW
802 M (2631 FT)

REGION: Southern   OS GRID: NY272005

Date:

Companion:

Weather condition:

Descent start time:

Descent duration

Finish time:

Difficulty:

☆ ☆ ☆ ☆ ☆

Views

☆ ☆ ☆ ☆ ☆

Ascent start time:

Ascent duration:

Peak time:

Rating

☆ ☆ ☆ ☆ ☆

Total Duration:

Total distance:

Total steps walked:

Notes

| THE OLD MAN OF CONISTON |

802 M (2633 FT)

REGION: Southern   OS GRID: SD272978

Date:

Companion:

Weather condition:

Descent start time:

Descent duration

Finish time:

Difficulty:

☆ ☆ ☆ ☆ ☆

Views

Ascent start time:

Ascent duration:

Peak time:

☆ ☆ ☆ ☆ ☆

Rating

☆ ☆ ☆ ☆ ☆

Total Duration:

Total distance:

Total steps walked:

Notes

....
....
....
....
....
....
....

HIGH STILE

806 M (2644 FT)

REGION: Western

OS GRID: NY167147

Date:

Companion:

Weather condition:

Descent start time:

Descent duration

Finish time:

Difficulty:

☆ ☆ ☆ ☆ ☆

Views

☆ ☆ ☆ ☆ ☆

Ascent start time:

Ascent duration:

Peak time:

Rating

☆ ☆ ☆ ☆ ☆

Total Duration:

Total distance:

Total steps walked:

Notes

LINGMELL
807 M (2648 FT)

REGION: Southern

OS GRID: NY209081

Date:

Companion:

Weather condition:

Descent start time:

Descent duration

Finish time:

Difficulty:

☆ ☆ ☆ ☆ ☆

Views

☆ ☆ ☆ ☆ ☆

Ascent start time:

Ascent duration:

Peak time:

Rating

☆ ☆ ☆ ☆ ☆

Total Duration:

Total distance:

Total steps walked:

Notes

....
....
....
....
....
....
....

STEEPLE
819 M (2687 FT)

REGION: Western

OS GRID: NY7116

Date:

Companion:

Weather condition:

Descent start time:

Descent duration

Finish time:

Difficulty:

☆ ☆ ☆ ☆ ☆

Views

☆ ☆ ☆ ☆ ☆

Ascent start time:

Ascent duration:

Peak time:

Rating

☆ ☆ ☆ ☆ ☆

Total Duration:

Total distance:

Total steps walked:

Notes

HART CRAG

822 M (2697 FT)

REGION: Eastern

OS GRID: NY369112

Date:

Companion:

Weather condition:

Descent start time:

Descent duration

Finish time:

Difficulty:

☆ ☆ ☆ ☆ ☆

Views

☆ ☆ ☆ ☆ ☆

Ascent start time:

Ascent duration:

Peak time:

Rating

☆ ☆ ☆ ☆ ☆

Total Duration:

Total distance:

Total steps walked:

Notes

RED PIKE

826 M (2710 FT)

REGION: Western

OS GRID: NY165106

Date:

Companion:

Weather condition:

Descent start time:

Descent duration

Finish time:

Difficulty:

☆ ☆ ☆ ☆ ☆

Views

☆ ☆ ☆ ☆ ☆

Ascent start time:

Ascent duration:

Peak time:

Rating

☆ ☆ ☆ ☆ ☆

Total Duration:

Total distance:

Total steps walked:

Notes

HIGH STREET

828 M (2717 FT)

REGION: Far Eastern

OS GRID: NY440110

Date:

Companion:

Weather condition:

Descent start time:

Descent duration

Finish time:

Difficulty:

☆ ☆ ☆ ☆ ☆

Views

☆ ☆ ☆ ☆ ☆

Ascent start time:

Ascent duration:

Peak time:

Rating

☆ ☆ ☆ ☆ ☆

Total Duration:

Total distance:

Total steps walked:

Notes

CRAG HILL
839 M (2753FT)

REGION: North Western   OS GRID: NY192203

Date:

Companion:

Weather condition:

Descent start time:

Descent duration

Finish time:

Difficulty:

☆ ☆ ☆ ☆ ☆

Views

☆ ☆ ☆ ☆ ☆

Ascent start time:

Ascent duration:

Peak time:

Rating

☆ ☆ ☆ ☆ ☆

Total Duration:

Total distance:

Total steps walked:

Notes

ST. SUNDAY CRAG

841 M (2759 FT)

REGION: Eastern

OS GRID: NY369133

Date:

Companion:

Weather condition:

Descent start time:

Descent duration

Finish time:

Difficulty:

☆ ☆ ☆ ☆ ☆

Views

☆ ☆ ☆ ☆ ☆

Ascent start time:

Ascent duration:

Peak time:

Rating

☆ ☆ ☆ ☆ ☆

Total Duration:

Total distance:

Total steps walked:

Notes

SCOAT FELL
841 M (2759 FT)

REGION: Western

OS GRID: NY159113

Date:

Companion:

Weather condition:

Descent start time:

Descent duration

Finish time:

Difficulty:

☆ ☆ ☆ ☆ ☆

Views

☆ ☆ ☆ ☆ ☆

Ascent start time:

Ascent duration:

Peak time:

Rating

☆ ☆ ☆ ☆ ☆

Total Duration:

Total distance:

Total steps walked:

Notes

....
....
....

....
....
....
....

STYBARROW DODD

843 M (2766 FT)

REGION: Eastern

OS GRID: NY343189

Date:

Companion:

Weather condition:

Descent start time:

Descent duration

Finish time:

Difficulty:

☆ ☆ ☆ ☆ ☆

Views

☆ ☆ ☆ ☆ ☆

Ascent start time:

Ascent duration:

Peak time:

Rating

☆ ☆ ☆ ☆ ☆

Total Duration:

Total distance:

Total steps walked:

Notes

GRASMOOR
852 M (2795 FT)

REGION: North Western

OS GRID: NY174203

Date: _____

Companion: _____

Weather condition:

Descent start time:

Descent duration

Finish time:

Difficulty:

☆ ☆ ☆ ☆ ☆

Views

Ascent start time:

Ascent duration:

Peak time:

☆ ☆ ☆ ☆ ☆

Rating

☆ ☆ ☆ ☆ ☆

Total Duration:

Total distance:

Total steps walked:

Notes

GREAT DODD
857 M (2812 FT)

REGION: Eastern

OS GRID: NY342205

Date:

Companion:

Weather condition:

☀ ❄ ⛈ 🌧 ☁

Descent start time:

Descent duration

Finish time:

Difficulty:

☆ ☆ ☆ ☆ ☆

Views

☆ ☆ ☆ ☆ ☆

Ascent start time:

Ascent duration:

Peak time:

Rating

☆ ☆ ☆ ☆ ☆

Total Duration:

Total distance:

Total steps walked:

Notes

....
....
....
....
....
....
....

DOLLYWAGGON PIKE
858 M (2815 FT)

REGION: Eastern
OS GRID: NY346130

Date:

Companion:

Weather condition:

Descent start time:

Descent duration

Finish time:

Difficulty:

☆ ☆ ☆ ☆ ☆

Views

☆ ☆ ☆ ☆ ☆

Ascent start time:

Ascent duration:

Peak time:

Rating

☆ ☆ ☆ ☆ ☆

Total Duration:

Total distance:

Total steps walked:

Notes

....
....
....

....
....
....
....

CRINKLE CRAGS

859 M (2818 FT)

REGION: Southern

OS GRID: NY248048

Date:

Companion:

Weather condition:

Descent start time:

Descent duration

Finish time:

Difficulty:

☆ ☆ ☆ ☆ ☆

Views

Ascent start time:

Ascent duration:

Peak time:

☆ ☆ ☆ ☆ ☆

Rating

☆ ☆ ☆ ☆ ☆

Total Duration:

Total distance:

Total steps walked:

Notes

WHITE SIDE
859 M (2831 FT)

REGION: Eastern

OS GRID: NY337166

Date:

Companion:

Weather condition:

Descent start time:

Descent duration

Finish time:

Difficulty:

☆ ☆ ☆ ☆ ☆

Views

☆ ☆ ☆ ☆ ☆

Ascent start time:

Ascent duration:

Peak time:

Rating

☆ ☆ ☆ ☆ ☆

Total Duration:

Total distance:

Total steps walked:

Notes

SKIDDAW LITTLE MAN

865 M (2838 FT)

REGION: Northern OS GRID: NY266277

- Date:
- Companion:

Weather condition:

- Descent start time:
- Descent duration
- Finish time:

Difficulty:

☆ ☆ ☆ ☆ ☆

Views

☆ ☆ ☆ ☆ ☆

- Ascent start time:
- Ascent duration:
- Peak time:

Rating

☆ ☆ ☆ ☆ ☆

- Total Duration:
- Total distance:
- Total steps walked:

Notes

....
....
....
....
....
....
....

BLENCATHRA
859 M (2848 FT)

REGION: Nothern

OS GRID: NY323277

Date:

Companion:

Descent start time:

Descent duration

Finish time:

Ascent start time:

Ascent duration:

Peak time:

Total Duration:

Total distance:

Total steps walked:

Weather condition:

Difficulty:

☆ ☆ ☆ ☆ ☆

Views

☆ ☆ ☆ ☆ ☆

Rating

☆ ☆ ☆ ☆ ☆

Notes

....
....
....
....
....
....
....

FAIRFIELD
873 M (2864 FT)

REGION: Eastern

OS GRID: NY358117

Date:

Companion:

Weather condition:

☀ ❄ ⛈ 🌧 ⛅

Descent start time:

Descent duration

Finish time:

Difficulty:

☆ ☆ ☆ ☆ ☆

Views

☆ ☆ ☆ ☆ ☆

Ascent start time:

Ascent duration:

Peak time:

Rating

☆ ☆ ☆ ☆ ☆

Total Duration:

Total distance:

Total steps walked:

Notes

....
....
....
....
....
....
....

RAISE

883 M (2897 FT)

REGION: Eastern OS GRID: NY342174

Date:

Companion:

Weather condition:

Descent start time:

Descent duration

Finish time:

Difficulty:

☆ ☆ ☆ ☆ ☆

Views

☆ ☆ ☆ ☆ ☆

Ascent start time:

Ascent duration:

Peak time:

Rating

☆ ☆ ☆ ☆ ☆

Total Duration:

Total distance:

Total steps walked:

Notes

....
....
....
....
....
....
....

ESK PIKE

885 M (2904 FT)

REGION: Southern

OS GRID: NY236075

Date:

Companion:

Weather condition:

Descent start time:

Descent duration

Finish time:

Difficulty:

☆ ☆ ☆ ☆ ☆

Views

☆ ☆ ☆ ☆ ☆

Ascent start time:

Ascent duration:

Peak time:

Rating

☆ ☆ ☆ ☆ ☆

Total Duration:

Total distance:

Total steps walked:

Notes

CATSTYE CAM
890 M (2920FT)

REGION: Eastern   OS GRID: NY348158

Date:

Companion:

Weather condition:

Descent start time:

Descent duration

Finish time:

Difficulty:

☆ ☆ ☆ ☆ ☆

Views

☆ ☆ ☆ ☆ ☆

Ascent start time:

Ascent duration:

Peak time:

Rating

☆ ☆ ☆ ☆ ☆

Total Duration:

Total distance:

Total steps walked:

Notes

....
....
....

....
....
....
....

NETHERMOST PIKE

891 M (2923 FT)

REGION: Eastern OS GRID: NY343142

Date: _____

Companion: _____

Weather condition:

Descent start time:

Descent duration

Finish time:

Difficulty:

☆ ☆ ☆ ☆ ☆

Views

☆ ☆ ☆ ☆ ☆

Ascent start time:

Ascent duration:

Peak time:

Rating

☆ ☆ ☆ ☆ ☆

Total Duration:

Total distance:

Total steps walked:

Notes

....
....
....

....
....
....
....

PILLAR
892 M (2927 FT)

REGION: Western

OS GRID: NY171121

Date:

Companion:

Weather condition:

Descent start time:

Descent duration

Finish time:

Difficulty:

☆ ☆ ☆ ☆ ☆

Views

☆ ☆ ☆ ☆ ☆

Ascent start time:

Ascent duration:

Peak time:

Rating

☆ ☆ ☆ ☆ ☆

Total Duration:

Total distance:

Total steps walked:

Notes

GREAT GABLE
899 M (1394 FT)

REGION: Western   OS GRID: NY211103

Date: _____

Companion: _____

Weather condition:

Descent start time:

Descent duration

Finish time:

Difficulty:
☆ ☆ ☆ ☆ ☆

Views
☆ ☆ ☆ ☆ ☆

Ascent start time:

Ascent duration:

Peak time:

Rating
☆ ☆ ☆ ☆ ☆

Total Duration:

Total distance:

Total steps walked:

Notes
....
....
....
....
....
....
....

BOWFELL
903 M (1394 FT)

REGION: Western   OS GRID: NY244064

Date:

Companion:

Descent start time:

Descent duration

Finish time:

Ascent start time:

Ascent duration:

Peak time:

Total Duration:

Total distance:

Total steps walked:

Weather condition:

Difficulty:

☆ ☆ ☆ ☆ ☆

Views

☆ ☆ ☆ ☆ ☆

Rating

☆ ☆ ☆ ☆ ☆

Notes

GREAT END

910 M (2984 FT)

REGION: Southern OS GRID: NY226083

Date:

Companion:

Weather condition:

Descent start time:

Descent duration

Finish time:

Difficulty:

☆ ☆ ☆ ☆ ☆

Views

☆ ☆ ☆ ☆ ☆

Ascent start time:

Ascent duration:

Peak time:

Rating

☆ ☆ ☆ ☆ ☆

Total Duration:

Total distance:

Total steps walked:

Notes

....
....
....
....
....
....
....

SKIDDAW
931 M (3054 FT)

REGION: Nothern

OS GRID: NY260290

Date:

Companion:

Weather condition:

Descent start time:

Descent duration

Finish time:

Difficulty:

☆ ☆ ☆ ☆ ☆

Views

☆ ☆ ☆ ☆ ☆

Ascent start time:

Ascent duration:

Peak time:

Rating

☆ ☆ ☆ ☆ ☆

Total Duration:

Total distance:

Total steps walked:

Notes

HELVELLYN
950 M (3117 FT)

REGION: Eastern   OS GRID: NY342151

Date:

Companion:

Weather condition:

Descent start time:

Descent duration

Finish time:

Difficulty:

☆ ☆ ☆ ☆ ☆

Views

☆ ☆ ☆ ☆ ☆

Ascent start time:

Ascent duration:

Peak time:

Rating

☆ ☆ ☆ ☆ ☆

Total Duration:

Total distance:

Total steps walked:

Notes

SCAFELL

964 M (3162FT)

REGION: Southern   OS GRID: NY206064

Date:

Companion:

Weather condition:

Descent start time:

Descent duration

Finish time:

Difficulty:

☆ ☆ ☆ ☆ ☆

Views

☆ ☆ ☆ ☆ ☆

Ascent start time:

Ascent duration:

Peak time:

Rating

☆ ☆ ☆ ☆ ☆

Total Duration:

Total distance:

Total steps walked:

Notes

SCAFELL PIKE
978 M (3209 FT)

REGION: Northern   OS GRID: NY215072

Date: _____

Companion: _____

Weather condition:

Descent start time:

Descent duration

Finish time:

Difficulty:

☆ ☆ ☆ ☆ ☆

Views

Ascent start time:

Ascent duration:

Peak time:

☆ ☆ ☆ ☆ ☆

Rating

☆ ☆ ☆ ☆ ☆

Total Duration:

Total distance:

Total steps walked:

Notes

....
....
....
....
....
....
....

Printed in Great Britain
by Amazon